The Hamrick generations, being a genealogy of the Hamrick family

S C. Jones

S. C. JONES (AUTHOR OF THIS BOOK) AND WIFE, EUNICE W. JONES, AND GRAND-
DAUGHTER, MAGGIE JONES

THE

HAMRICK GENERATIONS

BEING A GENEALOGY OF THE
HAMRICK FAMILY

BY
S. C. JONES
SHELBY, N. C.

1920
Edwards & Broughton Printing Co
Raleigh, N C

COPYRIGHT 1920
S C JONES
SHELBY, N. C

DEDICATION

To the memory of my loving mother, who departed this life on March 1, 1887, at whose knees I sat as a child and listened to many a recountal of the heroic struggles and vicissitudes of her early Hamrick ancestors whose exploits and undertakings account, in a large measure, for the sterling citizenship and well-founded progress of this immediate section, this book is respectfully and lovingly dedicated.

PREFACE

The author wishes to thus assure the readers of this work that he has made no effort to invite fame nor has he undertaken the furtherance of the art of authorship—rather it has been his in the compilation of data, facts and figures to give the direct and diverse ramifications of the several Hamrick generations and to show the honest strivings of them as early settlers and hardy pioneers.

No attempt has been made to perpetuate the fame of this great family in song and story rather the author has written, in plain and unpolished words, their rugged history. After all what could be more eloquent than the simple and hardy annals of the forebears of an honest and prosperous commonwealth whose efforts at building a sturdy citizenship have prevailed

Then too, no community is greater than the noble traditions and sentiments which it cherishes; so likewise is it with the individual. Wherefore, the writer prays the reader's leniency only as to grammatical construction for no apology is needed and none is offered for the record of achievements of the several generations herein enumerated.

Pardon is requested at this juncture for a personal allusion to the author: The author is by no means a finished scholar having attended the old field schools but a few months all told and going only at rare intervals, but in those rugged log temples—really monuments to the early efforts of each community's foremost educators—he at least learned the value of an education and was inspired to continue his eager search of knowledge Those facts being true the author has made no pretention at preëmpting the field of the rhetorician nor has he given his personal opinions; he has given the facts and the word-history as handed down. With these prefatory facts ever before you it is asked of you that you read the book with an eye single to acquisition of historical fact rather than grammatical precision

S. C. JONES.

HAMRICK GENERATIONS

The purpose of this book is to show the future generations the genealogy of the Hamrick Family The Hamricks are of German descent yet in their veins today flows the blood of the Irish, Scotch-Irish, English and French So it is hard to tell what are the leading characteristics of this people, whether the stubbornness of the Scotch, the quick temper of the Irish or the lack of humor of the English The spirit of the Hamrick of today has given him traits which characterize him as a law abiding, peace loving citizen. The Hamricks are like the children of Israel, they too cannot be numbered by multitudes The Children of Israel were like the sands of the sea, they could not be numbered by multitudes just so with the Hamricks In almost every state in the union the Hamricks are found some are farmers, some are lawyers, doctors manufacturers, merchants, jewelers, school teachers both in public and private schools, electricians, magistrates, legislators, congressmen, judges, preachers and in fact in every pursuit you find the Hamricks engaged

The Hamricks came to America in 1731 George Hamrick left Germany on account of his religion as he was not allowed to worship God according to the dictates of his own conscience, none daring to molest or make him afraid. He was a predestinarian Baptist or what we call the Primitive or Hard Shell Baptist and I have it from the lips of Old Uncle Berry Hamrick that all of the old set of Hamricks were Primitive Baptists and but few of them ever joined the church but all of them were ready and able to give a good reason for their hope of a better world beyond this vale of tears. The Hamricks are generally fond of out door life and are among the best farmers of the land today Some are poor and some are good livers while others are r.t. . . . .   Physically they are str. . . . . st order of the land. It has been repeatedly published that if you marry kinspeople that your offspring will be deaf, dumb, lame and blind, also mentally weak. If this be true then I make the assertion that there is not a Hamrick in all the land who would have sense enough to go to the mill and back by himself. Eighty per cent of the Hamrick generation have married their kin from the time they crossed the water. In olden times when a man went to look out a bride for himself the Lord told him plainly to go among his own kin, even his first cousins and we have the same God today that we had thousands of years ago. I have searched all the court records and I have only found six of this large generation ever indicted in the criminal court. They are honest law abiding people. Old David Webb once said that he was not afraid to sell goods to a Hamrick on credit and so instructed his son Hatcher to sell anything to the Hamricks on time and without mortgage. I have found some Hamricks who say they are not related to the other set of Hamricks "just across the river." I have searched the records and they show that only one Hamrick ever crossed the water. He left Germany in the year 1730 and landed at Philadelphia, Pa., in 1731, being seven months on the waters. He sailed from Rotterdam, Holland. The original name was Homrick, but today we spell it Hamrick. Now the Hamricks include and contemplate the Greens, the Blantons, the Bridges, Harrells, McSwains, Champions, Washburns, Wrays, Suttles, Bosticks, Ledbetters, Doggetts, Conners, Hughes, Magnesses. McBrayers, Webbs, Lovelaces and Williamsons. I don't think you will find any better people than found in this large generation of people. It has been in my mind for many years to write a history of the Hamrick generations or family, but I did not think then that they covered the land as water covers the sea. When I was young my dear mother would sit and tell all about her kin people and my grandmother, Peggy Hamrick, as she was called, would sit till midnight and tell all about her relatives. Neither of them had much education but very retentive minds and could tell one all about their family history. I have sat and heard them talk till I thought everybody was related to them but I never appreciated it till I began getting up this record.

I have a small book in which I began to take notes as long ago as 1870 and I had kept getting up a few more facts here and there until 1910. I went to work at this book with the intention of getting up this record of the Hamrick family but if I had known then what I do now I would never have undertaken the task   This has been one of the most stupendous jobs I have ever undertaken.   I have made two trips to Washington and four trips to Raleigh and have searched all records to find out this family and I am just now to "baker."

Old Aunt "Sookie" Hamrick, as she was called, gave me a great deal of information about the Hamricks.   Her name was Susanna Hamrick but they called her "Sookie" as a nickname.   Leander Hamrick has been a great help to me in this work also his brothers, John and Sidney.   James Y Hamrick, now dead, was also of great benefit to me, as he had a fine memory which enabled him to tell all about his relatives   But I owe the greatest part of my help to one whom I dearly loved, to-wit, Old Uncle Berry Hamrick   I have sat for days at a time and asked him many questions about the Hamrick generations: He could sit and tell one something new about them all the time and all about whom they married and where they settled   He said he had visited every old Hamrick who had ever come to this part of the country and he could tell one just what kind of a house each lived in and all about how they farmed.   Uncle Berry lived to be ninety-eight years old and had a splendid memory especially as to his kin-people.   The early Hamrick houses were made of logs and daubed with mud with two doors and two windows   One window at the fire place and the other at the back end of the house.   Some had what they called double cabins or two houses built together, with the chimneys reaching from one side of the house to the other or nearly so   They were generally from eight to ten feet wide and provided with what was called a pot rack, a pole up in the chimney to hang a pot on   Uncle Berry Hamrick said that many of their houses had no floors as there were no saw mills in this country at that time.   A great many of their houses had no shutters and the doors were filled with logs and poles to keep out the wild animals of which there were

J. Y. HAMRICK
DECEASED

a great many in those days. Some of them kept a fire all night in order to keep the wild animals from entering their houses

When George Hamrick left Germany he was an officer under the Kaiser, something on the order of Examiner of Passports for those going or coming across the ocean. Dr. W. C. Hamrick, of Gaffney, S C , has several letters stating that there is a large sum of money in Germany for the heirs of one George Hamrick who left there about the same time George Hamrick came to this country, but there is no credence to be to be put in such idle reports. This George Hamrick settled in what is now known as Germantown, Pa., and there is at that place a monument marking his last resting place He was the father of twenty-four children but I have failed so far to get more than seventeen of them and this book contemplates only three of them. Now I will give some of their names which are as follows· George, David, william, Moses, Thomas, John, Elijah, Greenberry, James, Reuben, Jane, Susanna, Hannah, Rebecca, Mollie, Mary, Sarah and Benjamin Three of his boys settled in Virginia their names were Moses Richard, George and Banjamin They died and were buried in Virgina but most of their children came to North Carolina about the year 1765

Benjamin's people all went on to Georgia and Alabama about the year 1830. Most all of Moses Richard's people went to Georgia and Alabama and some further West.

The Hamricks came here before there was any county as the records show that Tryon County was formed in 1769. four years after they arrived A great many of the Hamricks left here about 1830, or· later The Hamricks, Blantons. Greens. Bridges, Champions, Washburns, Bowens, McSwains all came across the ocean with George Hamrick The Blantons are of English descent George Blanton was the first Blanton that ever crossed the ocean Gabriel Washburn was from Germany, Henry Green came from England, Housand Harrell came also from England, William Champion was from France.

Now I will give as nearly as possible the places where these people settled, and where they were buried. I think it would be a good thing to have a meeting some time in the future and pay some respect to our beloved dead, as they were the pioneers and founders of this great section. I have visited all of the old graves of all these people mentioned above. There have been from seven to ten generations counting those that have passed away and those still living.

Samuel Hamrick entered land in 1797, one-half mile from Mt. Sinai Church and settled about two hundred yards from the old McSwain grave yard. In 1814 he entered land one-half mile east of Boiling Springs Church, just where George Robertson Hamrick lives. He was buried at what is known as the Katie Hamrick old place, two miles east of Boiling Springs Church.

James Hamrick, his brother, entered land at what is known as the Katie Hamrick old place in the year 1795, also in 1800.

Jones Hamrick entered lands at what is known as the Dr. Miller old place on the west side of First Broad river. He was brother to James and Samuel Hamrick. Jones went West about the year 1830.

Frederick Hamrick entered land in 1800 near the present Patterson Station. He went West about the year 1830. He was a brother to James and Samuel Hamrick.

Price Hamrick entered land in 1797, five miles west of Selby on what is now known as the Dock F. McSwain old place and was buried at the same place. His brother, Enoch Hamrick, entered land in 1800 on the west side of First Board river where Esley Davis once lived. He was buried down the river not far from William Lattimore's.

Nathaniel Hamrick entered land in 1797 on the waters of Hickory creek and First Broad river. This land is now owned by Major Sam Green. Nathaniel was buried at Old Buffalo Church, York, S. C. He was a brother to Price Hamrick.

Jeremiah Hamrick entered land just below the mouth of Hickory creek on the east side of First Broad river   He went to Alabama about the year 1830   He was also a brother to Price Hamrick

Henry Hamrick entered land on what is known as Bowen's river, just on the east side of the stream and now owned by John Crawford He was buried at Buffalo Church, York, S C.

Yelverton Hamrick entered land near Patterson Station and went West about the year 1830   He was also a brother to Price Hamrick

David McSwain came from Scotland and settled near the McSwain old grave yard on the east side of First Broad river at what is now known as the Buck McSwain old place.   He was the first white person buried in this part of the country   He was buried at the Mc-Swain old grave yard.

Next I shall tell how Bowen's river got its name   The Hamricks and Bowens camped on the river the first night they came into this country and Minor Bowen gave this creek the name of Bowen's river He gave nicknames to all people and places.   This river heads in Earl Station and runs south and empties into Main Broad river just below Buffalo Church, York, S C.

Minor Bowen settled on the west side of this river and just opposite where Henry Hamrick settled.

George Blanton entered land on the west side of Sandy Run creek, two and one-half miles southeast of Boiling Springs church.   He married Elvira Lee and was buried at his old place.   He was the first Justice of Peace in Tryon county appointed by King George of England on November 10th, 1769, the year the county was formed. Tryon county reached from the Virginia line and ran southwest to about where Charlotte is now located.   It struck the main Broad river where the two states now join.   All of this western country was Tryon county.

Gabriel Washburn entered land in Burke county but later moved to Rutherford county in 1820   He married Priscilla McSwain and was buried on the Berryman McSwain old farm.

Isaac Robertson entered land on the west side of Grogg creek near the Dock Rollins old place. He married Rebecca House and she made a trip every year to Virginia to see her people, walking there and back. At one time her sister came home with her and while here took sick and died and was buried at the Isaac Robertson old place. The heirs of Isaac Robertson raised money to put up a monument at his grave. Isaac Robertson was a Revolutionary soldier and belonged to Sharp's Company.

All of the Elijah Hamrick and wife Margaret McSwain children are eligible to join the Daughters of the Revolution through Isaac Robertson lineage. Margaret Hamrick's mother was Catherine Robertson, daughter of Isaac Robertson.

All of Moses Hamrick's people can join the Daughters of the Revolution through Isaac Robertson, as Moses Hamrick married Sarah Robertson, Isaac's daughter.

Henry Green came here with the Hamricks and married Nancy Reaves. He settled not far from Boiling Springs. Housand Harrell settled on the east side of Beaver Dam creek, one mile northwest of Beaver Dam church, on the north side of the Rutherford and Shelby road just below the Bill Bowen place and was buried at the Aletha Green place, near Ellenboro. He was elected to the Legislature from Rutherford county in 1804 and rode horseback to Raleigh and there bought his first saddle. He married Delphia Street.

William Champion settled on the east side of Main Broad river just below the mouth of Sandy Run creek. He married Mollie Hamrick and was buried at his old home place.

James Bridges settled one mile North of Mount Sinai church at what is now known as the Rufus Hamrick old place and was buried three hundred yards north of his old place. He was one of the first deacons of Buffalo Church. He married Rebecca Hamrick.

William McSwain married Susanna Hamrick and settled near his father, David, on the east side of First Broad river. He was buried at the McSwain old grave yard. His son, William, married Juda Moore. He served in the Revolutionary War in Brevard's Company. All of his descendants can join the Daughters of the Revolution through him. I do hope his descendants will erect a monument to his memory. What a nice thing it would be if the people would erect some monument to the last resting place of all these old settlers who first came into this country. Parenthetically I remind that I have traveled several thousand miles, mostly a foot, from house to house, spending several hundred dollars in getting up this work, but if I never profit further than that of having the satisfaction of having written the history of this great family's achievements I shall be content.

Now we have nineteen of the different families of this and Rutherford county. These people are among the very best in both counties. You may search the world over and you will not find any better people and as few backward ones in all the land. I have searched the court records and found but few of all these people who had any trouble with the courts.

Next I will write of the Blantons. They are good law abiding citizens and are among the very best people of this country. It is seldom you see their names in any court proceedings except when prescribed by business ends. They are good farmers and very thrifty in all their business affairs and undertakings.

The McSwains who are very numerous are very good farmers and law abiding citizens. One never sees their names in court unless perchance it is to obtain some right prescribed by law. They practice attending to their own affairs as much so as any family of people in the land.

Then there are the Greens. They are good honest people. Good farmers and law abiding and peace loving citizens. We should not look on the fault of one or two persons and judge the others by their

2

conduct but I am speaking of all these people as a whole, their record as a family is inspiring.

Next the Bridges They are good people, good farmers and law abiding citizens. honest in all their dealings with mankind I only found one or two by the name who have figured in the courts

Then we take up the Champions. They, too, are good people and it is seldom you see their names in the court records. They are good farmers, honest and upright in their dealings with their fellowman. Some of the old set were of very decided temperaments, but as a whole they are good people, doing well their parts.

The Wrays are also very good people and are among the best people in the country. I don't think I found a single Wray who had had any trouble in the courts. They are honest, sober and good farmers.

Then we take up the Suttles and we find them to be very fine people, honest in all their dealings, peace loving and law abiding citizens. They are among the best people of this country

Then here is the Bostic family. They are very good people although there are not many farmers among them, nevertheless they seem to be inclined towards serving the public They are honest and upright in their dealings. law abiding and peace loving citizens

The Harrells are also very good people and I never found any of them in court trouble. Some of them are very good farmers but taken as a whole they like public service and business life.

Then we take up the Washburn family. They are all very good people and have among them some very good farmers, but they, too, are inclined to be public men. They are honest and one seldom finds their names on the criminal docket

Then come the Conners. Most of these people are inclined to be farmers and are among our very best people. They give the courts very lit

Next we take up the Magness family These are good, law abiding, people honest and thrifty and boasting but few farmers

Then we take up the Mathenys and we find them to be among the very best people of the land, honest in all their dealings and good farmers This history covers every Matheny that ever came to this country. They are of Irish descent.

Next we speak of the Hughes. We find them good people and I never found but one of this name who ever gave the courts any trouble They are mostly farmers yet we find some of them engaged in public works.

Then we take up the McBrayer family. We find them to be among the best people of this country They are law abiding and peace loving people. They seem to be inclined as a whole to public life rather than to the farm, though some of them are successful farmers

Next comes the Webbs. We find them among our very best people. They also seem to be inclined to public service rather than to the farm I have never found any of their names on the criminal docket, although the name boasts some of the state's leading jurists.

Then we take up the Lovelaces These people are mostly inclined to farming and yet we see some of them in public life. They are good people. honest in all their dealings and I never found but a few of them on the criminal docket

Then we take up the Williamsons and we find most of them farmers They are among the very best people of the land. I never found many of the name on the criminal docket; they are kind and neighborly.

Then we take up the Doggetts and we find them good, law abiding and peace loving people, yet we find very few farmers among them, though they seem possessed lovers of stock and stock-trading

Then we take up the Byers family for nearly all of them are in this histor   . . . .   ing, yet

there are few farmers among them. Some have been public office
holders.

I have been very brief in speaking of all these different families
as they are all kindred characters and families. All are good people
—just as good as one finds in all the land. I have expended my best
efforts in compiling a complete history of the Hamrick generations,
yet it is not as complete as I should wish it to be. Then, too, I know
that mortal man is not perfect, so if you see a mistake in this work do
not make mockery of that which is intended to be good. Then, too,
think that the one who has labored so faithfully never went to school
six months in all his life. It was said that the writer could not get
up this history, but God being my helper, I am about completing it.
About ninety per cent of the present generations are Baptists and
Democrats. We were about to omit mentioning the Turners who are
concerned in this work. They, too, are among the very best people in
this country. They are mostly farmers, honest and upright in all
their dealings with their fellowman.

Now we come to speak of the condition of the country at the time
that these pioneer families came here. There were no white people
here at that time. Vast tribes of Indians inhabited this section. One
tribe six miles south of Shelby, near the Frank Young old place, one
south of Boiling Springs, one near Grassy Pond and one tribe near
Forest City. So you can see that the future looked very dark for
these people. Some of the early settlers herein mentioned were
killed by savages, some carried off and were never heard of again.

When the Hamricks came here they nearly all came in what is
known as a slide or sled, as such vehicles are called. When they came
to a river canoes were made of large trees and all of their possessions
put in these and taken across. Uncle Berry Hamrick said that he saw
many years afterward some of the sleds that brought them here at his
grandfather's, Samuel Hamrick's. When these pioneers came here
they cleared the land and cut out the younger growth. This
was don   and the large trees. After being

cleared the land was dug up with a mattock. Afterward they made a
crude plow stock out of a crooked tree, as nearly the shape of our
plow stocks of today as they could make them.   Then they had what
was called a mold board which they fastened to the plow stock and
made tight with a wedge. With this they plowed their lands.   Their
traces and lines were made of bark as there were no shops of iron in
this country at that time.   Most of them used oxen as the only
means of draft animals for cultivating their lands.   They took a
piece of crooked wood and hewed it out so as to form a yoke, the
traces were fastened thereto.   They worked their oxen from early
in the morning until late at night, then they turned them out to
graze.   They brought a little corn with them when they came to
this country.   Some they planted and some they saved for bread.
Most of the corn gave out before they could make a crop and
there were two or three months in which they had to go without
bread.   Naturally they suffered many hardships which to this
present generation would seem to be unbearable.   They killed wild
game which they ate.   They went to work early in the morning
and worked until about nine o'clock, then ate, then back to their
work where they remained until about four in the afternoon at which
time they would eat again.   They ate twice a day and only sparingly
at that. It was about ten years after they came into this country before
they sowed any wheat as they brought none with them.   But about this
time some people came from Virginia into this section who brought
wheat.   Governed by the Golden Rule, they divided this wheat, giv-
ing nearly every one a portion.   Now they threshed their wheat by
digging the ground down to the hard clay then took a maul and beat
the ground until it was very hard. Then they drove a post in the middle of this hole and put a shaft in the post, then hitched an ox or oxen
to the shaft. Then the wheat was strown all around and as the oxen
went around they trod out the wheat. Uncle Berry Hamrick said
the oxen which were used in treading out the wheat were never muz-
zled. Then they put the wheat into a vessel, two men got hold of a
sheet and they raised a wind by warping the sheet so as to fan the chaff
away.   They then ground the wheat in what is called a hominy mill

and sifted it through a single slade cloth.   Then the flour was made into bread without any soda or shortening.

The mill was made by taking a large tree and digging out a hopper in it about a foot deep and lined it with large headed nails   Then they took a large piece of wood and shaped it like a maul.   With it they beat up the corn.   Also they took another maul very much like the first one and fastened a large piece of wood to it, then tied a large rock to the other end of the pole, two men pulled up the beater and the rock pulled it back down   In this way the corn was ground They also made another sort of mill: This they fastened to limb on a tree and the limb helped them to manage the mill   They also used still another sort.   They took a large tree and dug a trough in one end and had a piece about four feet long under the other end   Then they turned the water into the trough and when the trough was filled with water the other end went downed and poured out the water. This made the heavier end come down so hard that it beat up the corn The corn which was finely ground they used for meal and the coarser was used for hommy.   A picture showing this old hommy mill is reproduced in this work.

FIRST CHURCH

A period of twenty-one years elapsed after they came into this country before there were any church buildings.   Buffalo Church in York county, South Carolina, was the first church organized in this part of the country   It was organized in the year 1786.   So you see these old settlers had no place to go to church but nothing daunted them.   They had meetings in private homes.   Joseph Camp was the first pastor of Buffalo church and James Bridges was the first named deacon.   His name is mentioned in this book.   Now I will come as near as I can in describing the old church building.   It was about forty feet long, twenty-five feet wide and about twelve feet high   The cracks were from four to six inches wide and were not daubed with mud like   two doors

OLD BUFFALO CHURCH HOUSE IN YORK COUNTY, S. C.—THE FIRST CHURCH IN
WESTERN NORTH AND SOUTH CAROLINA (BAPTIST).
DEDICATED IN THE YEAR 1786

in it and one window   A door was at each end and the window was in
the middle just over the "stand"   The house was covered with four
foot boards which were fastened on with wooden pins and then hung
over the rib poles.   Three feet of the boards were exposed.   The end
logs went to the top of the building   The building had a partition in
the back end and this space was reserved for colored people   The doors
and windows were hung on wooden hinges and the doors were fastened
with wooden latches.   I show in this book an illustration of this old
building   When the people went to church in those days they walked
back and forth.   They usually went to church on Saturday and then
walked back on Sunday   The women wore home spun dresses made
of materials which they had carded and spun by hand.   Their shoes
were made of home made leather over a very course last.   The heels
were as large as the shoe was wide   When they went to church the
women went bare footed and carried their shoes with them.   When
nearing the meeting place they sat down and put on their shoes   The
church had no chimney so they were kept warm by the fiery discourse
and arguments of the preacher who warmed up the whole congrega-
tion, and the fire burned the chaff, for it was salvation by grace alone
and this always burns the chaff.   The people walked from eight to ten
miles to hear the Gospel in those days and never seemed to get tired.
The benches in the church were logs split open, one log making two
benches   In 1789 Sandy Run church was built very much on the
same style as the Buffalo church   The deeds of both these old
churches were made to the Predestinarian Baptists as one can see by
the records

SLEDS

Almost everybody knows something about a slide or sled.   They
were made from eight to ten feet long with two runners   The front
ends were curved so as to run over rough places and stumps   Most
of the slides had standards   The slides, or sleds, were boxed up and
a whole family could get into one slide, or sled, and go to "preachin'"
or move f.. . .   . . Old Uncle James Ham-

rick, "Jeems," as he was called, would put his wife and five or six children in one of these slides, or sleds, and go to visit "Aunt Polly's" father, miles away.

THE TREAD MILL

In later years they made a pen of rails about four feet high and covered it over with rails. When their wheat got ripe they cut it and laid it into these pens, then took a hickory pole and beat out the wheat and cleaned it in the same manner as before stated. Later they invented a thresher which had wooden teeth in it. This thresher was run by confining a horse in a certain position and the horse kept tramping with his fore feet one foot upon one paddle and one foot upon another. By this process they operated the thresher which threshed out the wheat. I have seen this done, and still in some places they clean the wheat in the manner above stated, that is known as the treadmill.

SAW MILL

Now in those days they had what they called a whip saw. It was the only kind of saw mill the people had in those days with which to saw plank. This saw mill was mounted on a hill side with a scaffold built about 10 feet high. They hewed one side of the log and then lined it off with a blacking line, the lines just as far apart as they wanted the planks sawed. One man stood on the ground and another upon the top of the log in order that he might see the lines The man pulled up and another pulled down and in this way the planks were sawed. One person sat on the top of the log and drove a wedge in behind the saw so as to keep the saw from pinching. I have a finger now missing that was cut off by one of these saw mills while tightening the wedge. I show a cut of the old whip saw mill in this book. Two good men could saw from four to five hundred feet of lumber in a day, but it was hard work

FURNITURE OF THE SETTLERS

Uncle Berry Hamrick said that many of these old settlers had no beds when they came to this country They got some oak leaves and made a bed in one corner of the house. Some had what they called a bedstead. It had only one leg or post and it stood out in the middle of the room A hole bored in one side of the house and a hole in the bed post and a railing put into these holes, the other was made the same way and slats were laid across the railings, then the bed clothes were put on I have seen many of these old bedsteads in Mitchell and Yancey counties in this state. Bed curtains were hung on these beds, the curtains hung from the bed to the floor.

FLAX

Now I will tell you something about raising flax and the manner of preparing it for cloth The settlers planted the flax in a low wet place and when ripe it was cut and soaked in water for several days. Then it was dried and beaten with poles Next it was put into a break '; which was made with four slats on the bottom about three inches apart and about five feet long with three pieces on top as long as the bottom pieces. The top pieces went down through the bottom pieces and the flax was laid between them and when they came down together they broke up the flax into smaller workable bits. Then a paddle about three feet long and four inches wide and about one inch thick, sharp on both edges like an old fashioned butcher knife was used Next the flax was taken in one hand and the singling knife in the other and the flax was beaten to pieces Then what was called a hackle was used This hackle was made as follows. A piece of plank was used about four feet long and six inches wide, two inches thick and about one hundred sharp spikes made out of steel were driven into it. These spikes were about six inches long and about two inches apart with about four inches exposed. The flax was taken and slashed with these sharp spikes until it was cut very fine, following that it w   (\   ion of this old fashioned flax wheel is shown in this book. Then the flax was woven in a loom and finally made into clothing, both for men and women. The flax was never colored, being manufactured in the original color. I have seen many dresses made of the flax cloth, which was durable and lasting.

COTTON CULTURE

In the year 1815 the people began to raise cotton They planted it like corn, covering it with a plow In a few days they knocked the top soil off with a board. When the cotton came up a hoe was used and one person on one side and another on the other scraped the row from one end to the other. They never thought of cutting up a single stalk. They were very careful about cutting cotton up. When the cotton came up it was about six inches wide across the row. They made from two to three hundred pounds of seed cotton to the acre They never used any manure or any kind of fertilizer in those days After the cotton was gathered they picked off every particle of trash and picked out the seed with their fingers. Next they washed the lint as clean as they could Then it was dried, carded and spun. They used a reel, what was called a cracking reel. Some of these reels took one hundred and twenty threads to make a cut and five cuts made a yard Some had one hundred threads to the cut and it took six threads to make a cut. These reels did their own counting and when they got a cut they cracked off. This thread was taken and put upon a pan of winding blades and it was wound off on spools Then it was warped on a pair of warping bars. Next the thread was put on the beam of the loom, then through the harness and through the sleigh and around the small beams of the loom. Then the thread was woven into cloth. The cloth was colored and afterward made into clothing. A cut is shown of an old loom also the old cracking reel and winding blades in this book.

Some time later what was called a wooden cotton gin was invented. This gin was made with two wooden rollers, one on top of the other, and as close as they could be. These rollers had a crank on one side which was turned and one roller turned them both. So the rollers ran together and the cotton was fed in between these rollers. The seed came out on the same side.

I have it from Uncle Berry Hamrick that Samuel Hamrick invented the first wooden roller cotton gin in this country. I will also show a cut of the old wooden cotton gin in this book similar to the one exhibited at the museum at Washington.

WOOLEN CLOTH

Afterward sheep raising was undertaken and woolen goods were then made in very much the same way as the cotton goods. The woolen goods were always colored with dye flowers or walnut bark or some kind of coloring. Indigo was raised in those days and the people colored much of their cloth with it. A good spinner could card and spin a yard of thread a day, which was great speed for those days.

The raising of cotton entailed the use of what was called a hogshead. This was a large tree cut down and burned or cut out as thin as one could make it. A head was put in one end, the hogshead filled with cotton and packed with a press, on the style of an old fashioned cider press. Then the other end was planked up and a shaft put through the hogshead and shafts to the hogshead. Then a horse or oxen was hitched to it and the cargo carried to market at Columbia or Charleston, S. C. The tobacco was also carried to market in the same manner. Charleston and Columbia were the only markets in those days

WAGONS

The wheels of the first wagons were made of two pieces of wood, about eight inches wide and three inches thick and five feet long. They were put across one another. The axle tree was put into the middle of   ·   · · · de · ·m as thick as a large spoke and the rim was fastened to the spokes with wooden pins. I have seen many of these old fashioned wagons in the mountains of this state.

I tell you that the people had a hard time in those days. Just think for a moment of leaving father and mother, brother and sister and loved ones and going off into a strange unsettled land where no white people lived and where you expected to never see your loved ones again or hear any more from them in this life, for they never had a postoffice away back in those days. The first mail ever carried in the United States was in 1804, and the first stamps were used in the year 1847. So you see they never heard from home or loved ones any more after leaving them. They had no knives or forks, for the first ones manufactured in America were made in 1814. So they had to make good use of their hands in those days. A lot of them made wooden knives, forks, spoons and bowls. They also had wooden plates and wooden cups and saucers. Some time later they made all these things out of pewter and soapstone.

OTHER INVENTIONS

The first steamship crossed the Atlantic in 1819. It made its trip in about forty days. The first printing press made in America was in 1814. The first newspaper was published in Boston, Mass, in 1704. It was the Boston News, April 24th, 1704. This newspaper which was very small was printed by hand. The first railroad in the United States was in 1828. The first telegraph in 1835. The first sewing machine in 1846 was invented by Elias Howe. The first clock in 1836 was invented by Eli Terry. First electric lights in 1844. The first leather ever tanned in the United States was in 1795. The first matches were made in 1805 and cost ten cents for sixty matches. The first saw mill was in England in 1770. The first spinning jinny in 1767. It had only eight spindles. So you see that all these first settlers were deprived of every new invention that we are now enjoying.

Back in those early days almost all of the settlers made and used whiskey i: · ··· · ··· · · ··· ` ·· ···· ·· · · getting drunk. The preachers made and used it, also the deacons and church members. No one ever thought of slighting his brother in the church for drinking. I have it from the records that one of the best preachers in those days had a still and if he did not make whiskey himself he had it done. One Baptist preacher would still till meeting time, then go and preach, then back to the still that evening. That has not been more than sixty years ago.

Yes, they had fiddling in those days and one of the best preachers would go to church and preach and then go back home to play his fiddle. He never played such vulgar tunes as they do in these days. The fiddle was considered very creditable in those days.

They had no mourners' bench in those days at the church as the first mourners' bench was erected in 1835 by Lorenzo Dow. I have his book and he tells just how he got the mourners' bench started. Also the first protracted meeting. He went through this country in the year 1835. My mother said that she had heard him preach several times. He tried with all his might to get a stir among the people but failed. As he was going along one day near the state line in South Carolina he saw a little negro boy blowing an old tin bugle. His name was Gabriel. He said that he had never heard the like in all his days, that it almost made the hair rise on his head. He asked the little negro if he would go with him and blow the bugle for him. He finally persuaded the little negro to go with him. They both went on together before time for preaching. He got the negro Gabriel to climb the tree in the church yard and stay up in the tree until the crowd gathered, and when he heard the preacher come over the name 'Gabriel' for him to blow the bugle with all his might. When the preacher began preaching that night he tried with all his might to get the people's hearts astir but failed. Then Lorenzo Dow the preacher, came down with his fist on the book board as hard as he could and at the same time uttered these words "And what if you were to hear Gabriel sound his mighty trumpet tonight. What would you do?" "" . . . . trumpet with all . . . . . . both men

and women, both old and young The like was never seen   Lorenzo
Dowe had no trouble the next night in getting people to the mourners'
bench

THE OLD SETTLERS' COURTSHIPS

Well I will give a few courtships of some of the old Hamricks.
There was one Moses Hamrick who was going to see Sarah Robertson.
I suppose they had the match made up   However, one day Moses
was ploughing along when all of a sudden he decided that it was as
good a time for him to get married as he would ever have   He stopped
his plow, took out his horse and rode him off the field with his old
clothes on and rode about ten miles over to Isaac Robertson's, the
father of Sarah.   When he got there Sarah was down at the wash
place and he went on down there   When he got there he said, "Sarah
this is as good a time to marry as we will ever have." "Yes." said
Sarah, "But where are your clothes?" Moses says, ' I have them on."
"Well," said Sarah "If you are ready I am too   Where is the
preacher?"   Then Moses said, "He is up here."   They were both
married in their every day clothes.   This is no joke, it is the plain
truth for there are many witnesses to prove this statement.

Now I will give you the courtship of Old Uncle "Jeames" Hamrick,
as he was called   This he told me from his own lips   He was going
to his Uncle Billy McSwains' to see Aunt "Polly" and he said they
talked of marrying but he was like Ben Purdle, he could not get
his "blame" mouth off   So he went on in that way for months and
every time that he would go to Uncle Billy's he would try to get his
mouth to go off but it would not.   So one Saturday evening he went
again to Uncle Billy's and when he got there there was no one at the
house but Aunt "Polly '   He shook hands with her and as he took
hold of her hand he says "Polly would you have a body?" "Why yes,
Jeames you know I would."   This was all of their courtship for they
were married the next Sunday.   I suppose it does not make so much
difference as to the amount of words used as it does the love you have
for one a   l   ·   ,   l   ··   oved one

another it was Uncle "Jeames" and Aunt Polly I once knew a man who went to see a woman twenty years and married her, then killed her. A hundred years ago you never heard of any divorces. They married in those days for love, but today they seem to marry for the fun of it It has been recently published that forty per cent of the people that marry today get a divorce.

In the old days if a person made a debt the account was put on the books and it was good You can't say that today, for some people will sit in the Amen corner, sign a mortgage and then lie awake that night planning how to beat the other fellow out of the money.

The people back in those days were very poor farmers. They ran their rows up and down the hills. You can see some sign of their poor farming today. In a few years they had to clear up another field as the other land was washed away They never valued timber as worth anything There has been enough of good forest timber burnt up and destroyed in the field which if we had it today it would build almost every house in America. They cut the large pines down and burned them up on the ground and let some of them lie and rot They never studied about riches as do the people of today When you struck them on religious matters they were up-to-date Oh! what a change has taken place since forty years ago.

CAPTAIN MAGNESS

All of Benjamin Magness' descendants can join the Daughters of the Revolution through him. He was a captain in the Revolutionary army. He first married Elizabeth Mauney and then later married Sarah Walker Almost all of the Hamricks were in favor of the freedom of this country but there were only a few who took any active part, nor were they called upon to do so owing to the sparsely settled community.

Now I will give a little episode and I suppose it was true I have if from some of the younger set of Hamricks On one occasion one of the c   . . .   . ent to his brother Billy's and asked him to get up and give him some more booze. Billy told him plainly that he would not give him any more "You go home you have too much now," said Billy. Asa says, 'If you don't give me some whiskey I will jump into the well." "Go ahead," says Billy. In a few minutes they heard Asa hit the bottom of the well. The well was ninety-four feet deep. Billy jumped out to see and sure enough Asa was in the well. Then Billy had to tear down the beadstead to get ropes to pull Asa out. As they rolled him out he said "Roll, Billy Roll," and about every ten feet ' Roll, Billy Roll." So this became a by-word at log rollings "Roll, Billy roll." At another time Asa and one of his sons were going along one night. Asa had on a little too much booze again. He stepped off into a new well about twenty feet deep. His son told him "to stay there" until he went home and got some one to help him out. Asa turned a new leaf after that and professed a hope in Jesus. I truly hope he is at rest.

Old Uncle Berry McDaniel and my father were working at Elder Drury Dobbins' He set some whiskey on the table and said "Brethren, if any of you want a little whisky here it is, but don't drink too much." Now this is not mentioned to slander Elder Dobbins but only to show the use of whisky in those days. I am sure that no one esteemed Elder Dobbins any higher than myself.

The first person buried at Buffalo Church was a foreigner. He was passing the church yard with his gun when he saw a squirrel up one of the trees. He shot the squirrel and killed it. It lodged in the tree and he climbed up the tree and fell out and he himself was killed. They buried him at Buffalo Church in 1787, one year after the church was founded. No one ever found out the name of this man. I have this from old Uncle William Gaston, a member of the Buffalo Church. The first person buried at Boiling Springs was Sarah Hamrick, a daughter of Reuben Hamrick and wife, Hannah McSwain. She was buried in 1806. She was only two years old. The first person buried at Bethel was George Hamrick, son of Reuben Hamrick and Hannah McSwain. He was buried the 9th of May, 1882. The first person buried at D____ _____ ____ _____ ___ Ham-

3

rick and wife, Jane McSwain, on October 10th, 1881. The first person buried at Beaver Dam was Hosey Harrell, son of John Harrell and wife Susanna Washburn He was buried April 10th, 1871 The first person buried at Wall's Church was Octavia Bridges, daughter of Samuel Bridges and wife, Mary Winbrown, May 1st, 1877. So you see the Hamricks were the first in this country and the first to be buried at a number of the churches Warren Hoyle, son of Mr. F. L. Hoyle and wife was the first person killed in the European war from this county. He is a descendant of George Hamrick, who crossed the Atlantic in the year 1731. The Hamrick generations lost many people both in the Civil and European War. I had eight first cousins killed in one battle in the Civil War.

In 1881 a day's work brought fifty cents. Today it is worth from three to five dollars. Flour in 1881 was five dollars and fifty cents a sack Home killed meat twenty cents a pound; shoes from two to three dollars per pair; a suit of clothes eight to twelve dollars a suit.

Now I will give an example of the high cost of living. Consider the automobile and look at the enormous amount of money spent every day and night. If we only could keep an account of all the money spent for the above and say nothing about fruit stands and vaudeville shows and the like, then we would begin to see where the high cost of living comes in. I cut cross ties in 1886 for $8 00 a month and ate two meals a day. That was only thirty one cents a day, which would amount to fifty cents a day with two meals added. Now I have a son making thirty two dollars for four and one-half nights' work. So I don't see any use of complaining about the high cost of living. It all comes from extravagant living. Cotton in 1881 was nine cents per pound. In 1919 it was forty cents per pound, over four times as much as it was in 1881. Guano was twenty-one dollars per ton; in 1919 it was sixty-five dollars per ton

---

PUZZLING CONNECTIONS

No I . . . . le to work out
Since I . . . . e found five

families that had three great grandfathers and all three of them were brothers I have found five families that had three great grandmothers and all three of them were sisters   I have found three men whose grandfather and great-grandfather were brothers. I have found one man who had a first cousin and he and his first cousin's children were first cousins I found one man who was his grandchildren's own uncle I have found three people whose father was their uncle. Now can you find out these riddles?   They are all in the Hamrick generations I have found three sons, they and their father were brothers-in-law and yet-they have sense enough to go to mill and back by themselves.

Now if you see any families that are not represented in this book you may know that they left here many years ago   Elijah Hamrick married Milly McSwain and went West about seventy-five years ago. Hood Jolley and Richard Hughes both married Hamricks and went to Missouri many years ago. Some of the Bridges went West as did some of the Harrells. Also some of the Blantons, McSwains and Washburns journeyed westward

Now I have made an estimate of George Hamrick's descendants coming here from Virginia, and if the twenty-one other children multiplied like the three who figure in this book there would be at least three hundred and fifteen thousand of these people in one hundred and ninety years   So you see that they are as the sands of the sea Those three who are mentioned in this book have at least fifteen thousand descendants in one hundred and ninety-one years.   Records of twenty-one children I was unable to get into this work.   That looks like they are of Abraham's descendants.

There has been a great change in the last fifty years   Back then when passing a home you could hear the roar of the wheels and the cards and if you should go in would hear them talking about grandfather and grandmother, or some of their relatives   Today you will find one-fourth of the people talking politics and worldly matters   When you ask these people who was your grandfather or grandmotl   I   .   ..   . le since

I began this work who was your grandfather or grandmother and they could not say. I asked one grown boy who his mother was before she married and he could not tell. Back in those days the people used to visit one another and sit and tell their experiences and how they passed from law to grace. Today they are busy telling all about their corn and cotton and worldly affairs. You do not hear much said about religion, only what "they are doing for the Lord." The Bible says that many shall come in that day saying, "Lord, Lord, we have prophesied in thy name and in thy name done many wonderful works and in thy name cast out devils," and the Lord shall say, "Depart from me for I never knew you." I will let the readers of this book judge between now and fifty years ago as to religious matters. Back in those days they would sit and tell what great things the Lord had done for their souls. I have heard my father and mother tell their experiences and then old people would come in and they would sit up until midnight telling their experiences. Some telling of their loved ones gone on before to a better land than this

---

FIRST STORE

Now the first store in all this part of the country was near Gaffney, S. C., and was owned by Mike Gaffney and another man by the name of McCosten. This store was running in 1800. Only a very few articles were kept in this small store.

There was one Charles McSwain who was father of a boy about five years old. This boy was the reddest haired boy you ever saw. His father and mother thought very much of him. One day he went out to get something to make a fire and while away the Indians stole him. This was about the year 1800. As they thought so much of their red haired George they named the next boy born George. This boy was black haired. In 1812 the Indian war broke out and they re-captured their son from the Indians. So you see they had two boys named George, one red haired and the other black haired. Uncle Berry Hamrick sa___ ___ ___ ___ ___ ___ ___ ___ Neither father ever married. T___ ___ ___ ___ ___ ___ Thomas Moore

You have heard a great deal said about red headed George McSwain, this is what gave rise to the name.

There was one of this generation shot at the stake in time of the Civil War. His name was George Washington McSwain. He was one of the best men in this part of the county and one of the best soldiers in the Civil War. He got a letter from home that his wife was in a bad state of affairs financially and that she wanted him to come home at once. He got a furlough for thirty days and when the time was up he failed to go back on account of the conditions at home. When they came after him he was tried by court-martial and condemned to be shot at the stake. I will give a copy of his last letter that he wrote to his dear wife and children. It is very pathetic. Charles J. Hamrick and William Jasper Jones were drawn to shoot him. Charles J. Hamrick got out by being related to the condemned man and McSwain was killed before Jones had fired. They both said that George McSwain was one of the best men in their company. Whereupon comes the following letter.

CAMP NEAR ORANGE COURT HOUSE, VIRGINIA,
January 3rd, 1864

Hannah, Dear Wife and dear Children —

It is with painful regret that I have to say to you in way of writing my last letter that I ever expect to write in this world to you, as my days are but few that I have to spend in this unfriendly world, as I expect to part this life next Saturday by sentence of a general court martial to be tied down to a stake on that day, the 9th of this month, and shot to death with muskets. But little thought I had of this when I volunteered in the service of my country to protect my home and family that my life would be taken by my own people simply from absenting myself from my post with the view of protecting my little helpless children and affectionate wife who are as near and dear to me as my own life. Hannah, I was in very good heart and didn't think they would shoot me until yesterday morning. My sentence was read to me that I had to be shot next Saturday. It washed against me like the raging billows against a lonely rock in a sweeping storm, and I carefully examined myself and I feel well assured that when I leave the world that I will be better off than here. But to my little children and affectionate wife may the Lord prepare and fit them to meet me in heaven, for there will be no more parting of husbands and wives and dear children, but be rest forever. Hannah, dear wife, and dear little children, I never expect to see you any more in this life. My prayers are that you will meet me in heaven. Do the best you can and may God in his mercy rest and to with you forever Dear wife don t grieve nor trouble after me, for I feel that I am going to a better world and be at rest Then I won't be here to be punished any longer My afflictions have been severe, and I feel that I will be better oft when I leave this world Tell all my friends farewell for me, and farewell, dear wife, farewell, dear children Prepare to meet me in heaven I will close by saying, God bless my wife and little children Farewell

(Signed) GEORGE W McSWAIN

I will now give a list as nearly as possible of all members of the families herein mentioned who held public offices ·

Housand Harrell served in the Legislature from Rutherford county in the year 1804, and rode a horse bare backed to Raleigh, and there bought his first saddle

David Hamrick served in the Legislature from Rutherford county in 1834 As there were so many David Hamricks I will distinguish him from the others. His first wife was Rebecca Raney, his second wife Sarah McSwain.

William F. Jones served in the Legislature from Rutherford county in 1846.

Amos Harrell served in the Legislature from Rutherford county. in 1856.

Benjamin Washburn served in the Legislature from Rutherford county in 1858.

Charles Blanton was the first Sheriff for Cleveland county, elected in 1842 and served until 1852. He never carried a gun or pistol during his term of office.

George Green served as Deputy Sheriff under Charles Blanton from 1842 to 1852 He was then elected High Sheriff in 1852 and served until 1864. Then was elected again in 1864 and served until 1876. He served as County Treasurer for several years

James Y. Hamrick was the first Legislator for Cleveland county. He was elected in 1844 and again in 1848 and died during his second term of

Richard Champion was the first Clerk of Court for Cleveland county. Elected in 1842 and served until 1866, 24 years. The court was held at the old Evans House near Zion Church in this county.

John Blanton served as Sheriff of Rutherford county from 1880 to 1890.

His brother, Burwell Blanton, was one of the first trustees of the North Carolina College of Agriculture and Mechanical Arts in the year 1889, and his name is on the cornerstone of the college at Raleigh.

Greenberry Pruett served in the Legislature from Rutherford county in 1883.

Dr. John B Harrell served in the Legislature from Rutherford county in 1885

Capt Gold Griffin Holland served in the Legislature from Cleveland county in the year 1850.

William M Blanton served in the Legislature from Cleveland county in the year 1856.

James Y. Hamrick, Jr., served in the Legislature from Cleveland county in the year 1881. Also in the Senate in 1895. He was elected by the Legislature of North Carolina as Statistician from 1897 to 1901

James L Webb served in the Legislature for Cleveland county in 1883 and was elected state solicitor and served for several years. He was then appointed judge of the 16th Judicial District. He was appointed to this office by the Honorable Charles B. Aycock, Governor of North Carolina. He was afterwards elected by the people, and is judge up to the present time.

Wiley C. Hamrick served in the Legislature from Cleveland county in the year 1889. Also in the Senate from South Carolina in 1910.

Landrum L Smith served in the Legislature from Cleveland county in 1895.

Clyde R. Hoey served in the Legislature from Cleveland county in the year 1895   Also in 1901. Also in Senate in 1903.   He was appointed Assistant District Attorney in 1915 and held that office till elected to Congress December 16th, 1919.

Edwin Y. Webb, served in the Senate in Cleveland county in 1901 and was elected to Congress in 1902 and served until 1919 when he was then appointed by the Hon. Woodrow Wilson as Federal Judge for the Western District of North Carolina.

Oliver Maxwell Gardner was elected to the Senate in 1911 and in 1915   In 1916 he was elected Lieutenant-Governor of North Carolina pro tem.   He is now a candidate for Governor and I make the assertion that he will be our next governor.

Drury S Lovelace served in the Legislature from Cleveland county in 1909 and has been county commissioner for several years and has served as Justice of Peace for No. 2 Township for many years.

William Hamrick was a Justice of the Peace for forty-five years and it was said of him that he married more people than any other person in his day.   He was known as "Squire Billy " He got up a history of the Hamrick generation which he loaned to some of the deacons of Buffalo church and never got it back

Asa Monroe Lovelace has been Justice of Peace and County Surveyor of Cleveland county for many years.

Marshall Newton Hamrick was elected Sheriff in 1884 and served until 1894.

Albert B Suttle was elected Sheriff of Cleveland county in 1896 and served until 1908.

S C. Jones was appointed by the County Commissioners as Deputy Sheriff to wind up A B Suttle's tax   He served two years   He was elected Coroner of Cleveland county in 1912

Roy Blanton was elected Recorder of the Court of Rutherford county   ..   ..   during 1917

Willard Winslow Washburn served as Justice of the Peace for Cleveland county a number of years.

W. Posey Beam served as Captain in the Civil War; also served as County Surveyor for Cleveland county several years.

Dr. Lowson A Harrell was Captain in the Civil War and made a good captain.

Gold Griffin Holland was also a Captain in the Civil War.

S. M. Beam served several years as a Justice of Peace for Rutherford county.

Leander Holland served as Justice of Peace for Rutherford county several years.

T. C Eskridge has served as a Justice of Peace for Cleveland county and is now county coroner of this county.

J. H Beam served as Justice of Peace for Cleveland county for many years

James Beam served for many years as Justice of Peace for Cleveland county.

Joseph H Jones served as Justice of Peace for Cleveland county.

Wilson W Bridges served as Deputy Sheriff of Cleveland county for several years.

Thomas J. Holland served as Justice of Peace for Cleveland county.

John D. Putnam served as Deputy Sheriff for Cleveland county for several years He is now Road Commissioner of No 7 Township

John L. McSwain served several years as Deputy Sheriff for Cleveland county.

William B. Harrell served as Deputy Sheriff for Cleveland county for several years.

Lester Hamrick served several years as Deputy Sheriff for Cleveland county.

Lawson A. Bridges served as Justice of the Peace for many years for Cleveland county.

Burwell Benson Byers served as Justice of the Peace several years in Rutherford county.

Junius T. Gardner served as Mayor of the town of Shelby for twenty-two years. He was captain of the Cleveland Guards in the Spanish-American War.

Now I will give every reader of the book something to study about when they have nothing to do but talk about one another. Read the Golden Rule and do unto others as you would that they do unto you. Love your enemies, do good to them that hate you, pray for them that despitefully use and persecute you and say all manner of evil against you falsely for my sake

In speaking of a person's faults
    Pray don't forget your own,
Remember those in homes of glass
    Should seldom throw a stone

If we have nothing else to do
    Than talk of those who sin,
'Tis better to commence at home,
    And from that place begin

We have no right to judge a man
    Until he's fairly tried,
Then should we not like his company,
    We know the world is wide

Some may have faults   Who has none?
    The old as well as young
Perhaps we may, for aught we know,
    Have fifty to their one.

And though I sometimes hope to be
    No worse than some I know,
My own shortcomings bid me let
    The faults of others go

Then let us all when we begin
    To slander friend or foe,
Think of the harm one word may do
    To those we little know.

Remember, curses sometimes, like
    Our chickens, roost at home,
Then don't speak evil of others' faults
    Until we have none of our own

Oh! what a fine lesson is contained in the above piece of poetry if every one would heed it.

I've no mother now, I'm weeping,
    She has left me here alone,
She beneath the sod is sleeping,
    Oh! there is no joy at home
Tears of sorrow now have parted
    Her bright smiles no more I see,
All the loved ones too have parted,
    Oh! there is no joy at home

CHORUS

Weeping, lonely, she has left me here,
Weeping, lonely, for my mother dear

She was all this world to father,
    And she loved her children so,
But she is now at rest with Jesus
    Oh! I long, I long to go
Where my mother's singing glory
    And the angels hovering 'round,
All the saints of every nation,
    Oh! how sweet, how sweet the sound —*Chorus.*

Since my mother left me lonely,
    Death, that awful fiend, has come,
And has taken from me my father,
    I'm an orphan child alone.
Oh! when will the storm pass over,
    And the sun shine out again?
Then I hope to meet my father
    And my mother once again —*Chorus*

One by one my brothers going
    To a world unknown to me,
And my sisters too have parted,
    Their bright faces no more I see
Time will only tell the story
    When I too will meet them there,
But I hope and trust in Jesus
    All our troubles will be o'er —*Chorus*

I'm an orphan now I'm weeping,
    All my dear ones now are gone,
But I hope the time is coming
    When I'll meet them 'round the throne
Won't that be a happy meeting?
    Glory, honor to His name;
There will be no more sad parting
    In the new Jerusalem —*Chorus*

The above was composed by S. C. Jones on January 15, 1915, for the
Hamrick

I hear the cold winds sweeping,
  Through every vale and tree,
Where my dear father's sleeping
  Away from home and me

Tears from my eyes are falling
  Deep sorrow shades my brow,
Cold in the grave he is sleeping,
  I have no father now

He was a loving father,
  A friend to all his foes;
He is now at rest with Jesus,
  Where all good people go

Kind friends will cease to greet him,
  For death has paled his brow,
I want to go and meet him,
  I have no father now

I see the darkness hovering
  Around my mother's grave;
But, oh! that lonesome cottage,
  No mortal one can crave

I've thought of my dear mother
  With tears upon my brow,
For she has gone and left me,
  I have no mother now

Sad was the hour of parting;
  She said in words so sweet
"My loved ones, now I'm dying,
  In glory we shall meet."

I hope to meet my parents
  Upon the eternal shore,
And there we'll dwell together,
  Where parting is no more

I had a little brother,
  The idol of my heart;
But he, too, now is sleeping;
  How sad it is to part.

The resurrection morning,
  When all the saints shall rise,
They all shall live with Jesus,
  So far above the skies

I had a loving sister,
  To me she was so kind,
But now I am so lonely,
  For I am left behind

But God saw fit to call her,
  Farewell, we all must part,
And meet dear ones in glory,
  And there no more to part

This was composed by S. C. Jones on March 31, 1916, for my dear cousin, Fannie Hamrick, Dothan, Ala. It is sung to the old tune of "Complainer."

One night, while I was all alone,
  A dark and lonesome sigh,
My time on earth I thought had come,
  And I was bound to die
My sins all in a moment rose,
  Like a tumult in the skies
I tried the law and no mercy there
  For rebels such as I

My mother then began to sing,
  But to a dying man,
I thought that in a moment I
  Should surely with Him stand
To hear my just and certain doom,
  Like a criminal at the bar,
Pleading for mercy though death be just,
  Lord save, was my desire.

That night has often come to me,
  Although my mother's gone,
I still can hear her voice ascend
  The great celestial throne
I thought her prayers were then too late
  For this poor sinful man,
Not knowing then that I had come
  Where every poor sinner must come

I don't believe one wants to be
  In such a dreadful state,
Oh, brethren, sisters, one and all,
  Oh, won't you here relate,
If it had then been left to you,
  Let the bitter cup pass on,
And you had been as you were before,
  That you had not been born

Ye weary, heavy-laden souls,
  Who are oppressed sore,
Ye travelers through this wilderness
  To Canaan's peaceful shore;
Come tell me is it thus with you,
  And is my story true?
For if you are saved, it is by grace,
  There is nothing you can do.

It was one night upon my bed
  This burden rolled away;
It's brought my weary hungry soul
  Up to the present day
Oh, what a happy thought is this,
  To hear the sinner tell,
How Jesus in His mercy has
  Saved his poor soul from hell

I started out one summer day,
  I thought a home to find,
I found a place they called the church,
  It did not ease my mind
My troubles then arose anew,
  I then began to search,
I hoped that Jesus in His love
  Showed me the only church

We are often like the lonesome dove,
  That mourns her absent mate;
From hill to hill, from grove to grove,
  Her woes she doth relate
But Canaan just before us lies,
  Sweet spring is coming on,
A few more beating winds and rains,
  And winter will be gone

Oh, for a breeze of heavenly love,
  To waft my soul away
To that celestial world above,
  Where pleasures ne'er decay
It's far beyond the glittering sun,
  That blissful, heavenly dove,
I hope to dwell when time is done,
  And praise my God above.

Oh, who can tell of a lonesome dove,
  While mourning her love to know,
Her mate is taken away and gone,
  And she is left alone;
Just so poor sinners sometimes are,
  When Jesus hides His face,
But when His blessed voice they hear,
  "My child you are saved by grace"

The above was composed by S C Jones, July 12, 1876, on his experience

In slumbering sleep I lay
　One night upon my bed,
A vision very strange
　Or a thought came to my head,
I dreamed of the day of doom,
　And doubtless it had come,
And Christ Himself was there
　To summons old and young

And I myself was called,
　With trumpets loud and shrill,
Saying, "Every soul must rise,
　Be their sentence good or ill "
With fear I trembling stood,
　And little did I know,
But I knew Christ's mercy's great,
　And I trusted and did go

I had not been there long
　Before old Satan came,
Dressed up in his filthy robe,
　And my sins he brought along,
He laid them before the Lord,
　And said I was his own,
My sins being full and great,
　For 'twas many I had done

Then said our blessed Lord,
　"I soon will end the strife,
I'll see if the sinner's name
　Is not in the book of life '
The book of life was brought,
　And many leaves unfold,
And the sinner's name was there,
　And the letters written in gold.

Then said our blessed Lord,
　"Oh, stay, old Satan, stay,
For the sinner's name is here,
　And his sins are washed away "
Then murmuring Satan stood
　All in a dismal plight,
And said unto the Lord,
　"Your indictments are not right "

Then said our blessed Lord,
　"Oh, why, old Satan, why?
Satan, you know right well
　For poor sinners I did die
I died to redeem my bride,
　Who once was lost by thee,
　　　It (   ) out
　　　　I   (   ) pure

THE GOSPEL CHURCH

Well, wife, I've found the model church,
    And worshipped there today;
It made me think of good old times
    Before my hair was gray
The meeting house was finer built
    Than they were years ago,
But then I found when I went in
    It was not built for show.

The sexton did not sit me down
    Away back by the door,
He knew that I was old and deaf,
    And saw that I was poor
He must have been a Christian man,
    He led me boldly through
The crowded aisle of that grand church
    To find a pleasant pew

You should have heard that singing, wife,
    It had the old-time ring,
The preacher said with trumpet voice,
    "Let all the people sing"
Old Coronation was the tune,
    The music upward rolled,
Until I thought the angel choir
    Struck all their harps of gold

My deafness seemed to melt away,
    My spirit caught the fire,
I joined my feeble, trembling voice
    With that melodious choir
And sang as in my youthful days,
    "Let angels prostrate fall,
Bring forth the royal diadem,
    And crown him Lord of all"

I tell you, wife, it did me good
    To sing that hymn once more;
I felt like some wrecked mariner
    Who gets a glimpse of shore
I almost want to lay aside
    This weather-beaten form,
And anchor in the blessed port
    Forever from the storm

'Twas not a flowery sermon, wife,
    But simple gospel truth,
It fitted humble men like me,
    It suited hopeful youth
To win the sin-sick souls to Christ
    The earnest preacher tried,
He preached not of himself or creed,
    But Jesus crucified

Dear wife, the toil will soon be o'er,
    The victory soon be won,
The shining land is just ahead,
    Our race is nearly run
We are nearing Canaan's happy shore,
    Our home so bright and fair,
Thank God we'll never sin again,
    There'll be no sorrow there

4

COUNTY HISTORIES

Alamance—Alamance County was formed in 1849 from Orange. The name is supposed to have been derived from an Indian word meaning blue clay. The County gets its name from Alamance Creek, On the banks of which were fought the battle between the Colonial Troops under Gov. Tryon and the Regulators, May the 16th, 1771. The county seat is Graham.

Alexander.—Alexander County was formed in 1847 from Iredell, Caldwell and Wilkes. Was named in honor of William J. Alexander, of Mecklenburg County, several times a member of the Legislature and speaker of the House of Commons. The county seat is Taylorsville.

Alleghany.—Alleghany County was formed in 1859 from Ashe. The name is derived from an Indian tribe in the limits of North Carolina. Sparta is the county seat. Alleghany voted with Ashe until 1866.

Anson—Anson County was formed in 1749 from Bladen. Was named in honor of Lord George Anson, a celebrated English Admiral who circum-navigated the globe. He lived for a while on the Pee Dee in South Carolina. In 1761 he was given the honor of bringing to her marriage with King George III, Charlotte, Princess of Mecklenburg, for whom Mecklenburg County is named. The county seat is Wadesboro

Ashe—Ashe County was formed in 1799 from Wilkes. Was named in honor of Samuel Ashe of New Hanover, brother of General John Ashe. Samuel Ashe was a Revolutionary patriot, one of the first judges of the State, and afterwards governor. The county seat is Jefferson

Beaufort—Beaufort County was formed in 1705 from Bath. Was first called Archdale and name changed to Beaufort about 1712. It was nar̄ ____ ____ ____ of H___ Somer___ Duke of Beaufort, who in 1709 be___ ____ ____ ___ ____ proprietor of the Carolina. He purchased the share originally owned by the Duke of Albemarle.   The county seat is Washington.

Bertie.—Bertie County was formed in 1722 from Bath.   Was named in honor of James and Henry Bertie, Lord Proprietors, who in 1728 owned the shares of Lord Clarendon.   The county seat is Windsor.

Bladen.—Bladen County was formed in 1734 from Bath.   Was named in honor of Martin Bladen, one of the members of the Board of Trade which had charge of colonial affairs.   The county seat is Elizabethtown.

Brunswick.—Brunswick was formed in 1764 from New Hanover and Bladen   Was named in honor of the famous house of Brunswick, of which the four Georges, kings of England, were members. The county seat is Southport.

Buncombe —Buncombe County was formed in 1791 from Burke and Rutherford.   Was named in honor of Col Edward Buncombe, a Revolutionary soldier, who was wounded and captured at the battle of Germantown, Oct 4th, 1777, and died a parole prisoner, May 1778, in Philadelphia.   Col Buncombe lived in Tyrrell County   He was noted for his hospitality   Over the door of his house were these lines: "Welcome all to Buncombe Hall"

Burke.—Burke County was formed in 1777 from Rowan County. Was named in honor of Dr Thomas Burke, member of the Continental Congress and Governor of North Carolina   The county seat is Morganton.

Bute —Bute County was formed in 1764 from Grandville.   Was named for John Stuart, Earl of Bute, one of the principal Secretaries of State, also first lord of the treasury under King George III, over which monarch he exercised a dominant influence.   The Earl became very unpopular with the Americans, and in 1778 the General Assembly of North Carolina passed an act which wiped Bute County from the map, dividing its territory into new counties called Warren

OLD-FASHIONED WHIP SAW USED IN EARLY MANUFACTURE OF LUMBER.
(SEE PAGE 25)

and Franklin, after the Revolutionary patriots, Joseph Warren and Benjamin Franklin.

Cabarrus —Cabarrus County was formed in 1792 from Mecklenburg   Was named in honor of Stephen Cabarrus, of Edenton, several times member of the Legislature and often speaker of the House of Commons   The county seat is Concord.

Caldwell —Caldwell County was formed in 1841 from Burke and Wilkes.   Was named in honor of Joseph Caldwell the first President of the University of North Carolina.   He was one of the first and strongest advocates of the public school system, and of the railroad through the center of the state from Morehead City to Tennessee.   Lenoir is the county seat.

Camden.— Camden County was formed in 1777 from Pasquotank. Was named in honor of the learned Englishman, Charles Pratt, Earl of Camden, who was one of the strongest friends of the Americans in the British Parliament.   He took their side in a dispute over taxation without representation.   The county seat is Camden Court House

Carteret —Carteret County was formed in 1722 from Bath   Was named in honor of Sir John Carteret, afterwards in 1744 Earl Granville, one of the Lord Proprietors, when the other Lord Proprietors sold their shares to the king in 1728, Cartaret was induced to sell An immense tract of land in North Carolina was laid off as his share in 1744.   It was called Granville District and was the cause of a great deal of trouble.   He lost it by confiscation when the Revolution freed North Carolina from the British rule   Beaufort is the county seat.

Caswell —Caswell County was formed in 1777 from Orange   Was named in honor of Richard Caswell, member of the First Continental Congress, first Governor of North Carolina after the Declaration of Independence   Six times re-elected Governor and Major-General in the Revolutionary Army   Yanceyville is the county seat

Catawba   Catawba County was formed in 1842 from Lincoln

Was named after a tribe of Indians which dwelt in that section of the State. Newton is the county seat Catawba County voted with Gaston and Lincoln until 1854.

Chatham —Chatham County was formed in 1770 from Orange. Was named in honor of the great Englishman who won for England all of French America and was the most eloquent defender of the American cause in the British Parliament during the Revolution, William Pitt, Earl of Graham Pittsboro is the county seat.

Cherokee.—Cherokee County was formed in 1839 from Macon. Was named after an Indian tribe which still dwells in that section of the State Murphy is the county seat.

Chowan.— Chowan County was formed in 1672 from Albemarle. Was named for an Indian tribe dwelling in the northeastern part of the State when the English first came to North Carolina Edenton is the county seat

Clay — Clay County was formed in 1861 from Cherokee. Was named in honor of the great orator and statesman Henry Clay. Hayesville is the county seat. Prior to 1868 Clay voted with Cherokee

Cleveland —Cleveland County was formed in 1841 from Rutherford and Lincoln. Was named in honor of Col Benjamin Cleveland, a noted partisan leader on the western North Carolina frontier in the Revolution, and one of the heroes of King's Mountain Shelby is the county seat.

Columbus.—Columbus County was formed in 1808 from Bladen and Brunswick Was named in honor of the discoverer of the new world Whiteville is the county seat.

Craven.—Craven County was formed in 1712 from Bath Was named in honor of William, Lord Craven, one of the Lord Proprietors of Carolina. New Bern is the county seat.

Cumbe ... ... formed in 1754 from

Bladen. Was named in honor of William Augustus, Duke of Cumberland, second son of King George II Cumberland was commander of the English Army at the battle of Culloden, in which the Scotch Highlanders were so badly defeated Many of them came to America and their principal settlement was at Cross Creek in Cumberland County. Fayetteville is the county seat.

Currituck —Currituck County was formed in 1672 from Albemarle. Was named after an Indian tribe Currituck Court House is the county seat.

Dare.—Dare County was formed in 1870 from Currituck, Tyrrell and Hyde Was named in honor of Virginia Dare, the first English child born in America Manteo is the county seat.

Davidson —Davidson County was formed in 1822 from Rowan. Was named in honor of General William Lee Davidson, a soldier of the Revolution, who was killed at the battle of Cowan's Ford, when General Green retreated across North Carolina before Cornwallis in 1781. He stationed some troops under General Davidson at Cowan's Ford over the Catawba River to delay the British Army The British attacked the Americans, killed General Davidson, and forced the passage The United States has erected a monument in his honor on Guilford Battle Ground Lexington is the county seat.

Davie —Davie County was formed in 1836 from Rowan Was named in honor of William R. Davie, distinguished as a soldier of the Revolution, member of the Federal Convention of 1787, Governor of North Carolina. Special Envoy Extraordinary and Minister Plenipotentiary to France, father of the University of North Carolina Mocksville is the county seat.

Dobbs.—Dobbs County abolished in 1791.

Duplin —Duplin County was formed in 1749 from New Hanover. Was named in honor of George Henry Hay, Lord Duplin, an English nobleman Kenansville is the county seat

Durham - Durham County was formed in 1881 from Orange and

Wake. Was named after the town of Durham, a thriving manufacturing city. Durham is the county seat.

Edgecombe—Edgecombe County was formed in 1735 from Bertie. Was named in honor of Richard Edgecombe, who became Baron Edgecombe in 1742, an English Nobleman and a Lord of the Treasury. Tarboro is the county seat

Forsyth—Forsyth County was formed in 1849 from Stokes. Was named in honor of Col Benjamin Forsyth, U. S A., a citizen of Stokes County, who was killed on the Canadian frontier on June 28th, 1814, during the second war with Great Britain Winston-Salem is the county seat.

Franklin—Franklin County was formed in 1779 from Duke. Was named in honor of Benjamin Franklin Louisburg is the county seat.

Gaston—Gaston County was formed in 1846 from Lincoln. Was named in honor of Judge William Gaston, member of Congress and Justice of the Supreme Court of North Carolina Dallas is the county seat. From 1846 to 1852 Gaston voted with Lincoln and Catawba.

Gates—Gates County was formed in 1778 from Chowan, Perquimans and Hertford Was named in honor of General Horatio Gates, who commanded an American army at the battle of Saratoga At this battle an entire British army was captured, but General Gates contributed nothing to that success It was regarded as one of the most important battles in the history of the world Gatesville is the county seat.

Glasgow—(Abolished in 1799)

Graham—Graham County was formed in 1872 from Cherokee. Was named in honor of Gov. William A Graham, United States Senator, Governor of North Carolina, Secretary of the Navy, Confederate State Senator Robbinsville is the county seat Graham voted with Cherokee

Granville—Granville County was formed in 1746 from Edgecombe. Was named in honor of John Carteret, Earl of Granville, who owned the Granville District. He was prime Minister under King George II, and a very brilliant man. Oxford is the county seat.

Greene.—Greene County was formed in 1799 from Glasgow. Was named in honor of General Nathaniel Greene, Washington's right hand man. Next to Washington, General Greene is regarded as the greatest soldier of the Revolution. He fought the battle of Guilford Court House and saved North Carolina from the British. Snow Hill is the county seat.

Guilford.—Guilford County was formed in 1770 from Rowan and Orange. Was named in honor of Francis North, Earl of Guilford, an English nobleman. He was the father of Lord North who was Prime Minister under King George III during the Revolution. Lord North afterwards succeeded his father as Earl of Guilford. Greensboro is the county seat

Halifax—Halifax County was formed in 1754 from Edgecombe. Was named in honor of George Montague Dunk, Earl of Halifax, President of the Board of Trade which had control of the colonies before the Revolution. Halifax is the county seat.

Harnett—Harnett County was formed in 1855 from Cumberland. Was named in honor of Cornelius Harnett, eminent Revolutionary patriot, President of the Provincial Council, President of the Council of Safety, Delegate to the Continental Congress. Author of the Halifax Resolution of April 12, 1776. Lillington is the county seat. Harnett voted with Cumberland until 1865.

Hawkins.—(Now in Tennessee.)

Haywood.—Haywood County was formed in 1808 from Buncombe. Was named in honor of John Haywood, who for forty years, 1787-1827, was the popular Treasurer of the State. Waynesville is the county seat

Henderson —Henderson county was formed in 1838 from Buncombe. Was named in honor of Leonard Henderson, Chief Justice of the Supreme Court of North Carolina   Hendersonville is the county seat.

Hertford.—Hertford County was formed 1759 from Chowan, Bertie, and North Hampton   Was named in honor of Francis Seymour Conway, Marquis of Hertford, an English Nobleman.   He was a brother of General Conway, a distinguished British soldier and member of Parliament, who favored the repeal of the Stamp Act.   The word Hertford is said to mean Red Ford.   Winston is the county seat.

Hoke.—Hoke County was formed in 1911 from Cumberland and Robeson.   Was named in honor of Robert S. Hoke, of North Carolina, Major-General in the Confederate States Army.   Raeford is the county seat.

Hyde —Hyde County was formed in 1705 from Bath   Called Wickham until about 1712   Named Hyde in honor of Gov Edward Hyde, of North Carolina, a grandson of the Earl of Clarendon.   The Earl was one of the Lord Proprietors.   Gov. Hyde was a first cousin of Queen Anne   County seat is Swan Quarter

Iredell.—Iredell County was formed in 1788 from Rowan. Named in honor of James Iredell, of Edenton, who was one of the foremost lawyers of the State   In 1788 and 1789 he was one of the leaders in the State in advocating the adoption of the Constitution of the United States   His speeches in the Convention of 1788 at Hillsboro were among the ablest delivered by any of the advocates of the Constitution   Washington appointed him in 1790 a Justice of the Supreme Court of the United States.   The County seat of Iredell County is Statesville.

Jackson —Jackson County was formed in 1851 from Haywood and Macon   Named in honor of Andrew Jackson, who was born in Mecklenburg County   (The site of his birthplace is now in Union)

He won the brilliant victory over the British at New Orleans in 1815, and was twice elected President of the United States   The county seat is Webster.

Johnston.—Johnston County was formed in 1746 from Craven. Afterwards parts of Duplin and Orange were added   Was named in honor of Gabriel Johnston, Governor of North Carolina from 1734 to 1752   The county seat is Smithfield

Jones—Jones County was formed in 1778 from Craven, was named in honor of Willie Jones, of Halifax   He was the leading patriot of the Revolution, was President of the Council of Safety, and was opposed to the adoption of the Constitution of the United States   It was due to his influence that the Constitution at the Convention of 1788 rejected it   The county seat is Trenton.

Lee.—Lee County was formed in 1907 from Chatham and Moore, named in honor of Robert E. Lee.   The county seat is Laurinburg.

Lenoir.—Lenoir County was formed in 1791 from Dobbs and Craven, was named in honor of General William Lenoir, one of the heroes of King's Mountain   Kinston is the county seat

Lincoln—Lincoln County was formed in 1779 from Tryon   was named in honor of Col Benjamin Lincoln, General of the Revolution, whom Washington appointed to receive the sword of Lord Cornwallis at the surrender of Yorktown   Lincolnton is the county seat

Macon.—Macon County was formed in 1828 from Haywood, was named in honor of Nathaniel Macon, Speaker of the National House of Representatives, United States Senator, President of the Constitutional Convention of 1835.   The county seat is Franklin.

Madison.—Madison County was formed in 1851 from Buncombe and Yancey, was named in honor of James Madison, fourth President of the United States   The county seat is Marshall.

Martin.—Martin County was formed in 1774 from Halifax and

Tyrrell, was named in honor of Josiah Martin the last Royal Governor of North Carolina It is probable that this name would have been changed like those of Dobbs and Tryon, but for the popularity of Alexander Martin, who was Governor in 1782 and again in 1790 The county seat is Williamston

McDowell.— McDowell County was formed in 1842 from Rutherford and Burke, was named in honor of Col Joseph McDowell, an attractive officer of the Revolution McDowell voted with Rutherford and Burke until 1854. Marion is the county seat.

Mecklenburg—Mecklenburg County was formed in 1762 from Anson, was named in honor of Princess Charlotte, of Mecklenburg, Queen of George III, King of England The county seat, Charlotte, one of the prettiest cities in the State, was also named in her honor Mecklenburg County was the scene of some of the most stirring events of the Revolution Charlotte is the county seat

Mitchell.—Mitchell County was formed in 1861 from Yancey, Watauga, Caldwell, Burke and McDowell, was named in honor of Dr. Elisha Mitchell, a professor in the University of North Carolina. While on an exploring expedition on Mt Mitchell, the highest peak East of the Rocky Mountains, Dr. Mitchell fell from a high peak and was killed His body was buried on the top of this lofty mountain The county seat is Bakersville. Mitchell County voted with Yancey County until 1868.

Montgomery—Montgomery County was formed in 1778 from Anson, was named in honor of the brave General Richard Montgomery, who lost his life at the battle of Quebec in 1775 while trying to conquer Canada. The county seat is Troy

Moore—Moore County was formed in 1784 from Cumberland, was named in honor of Capt Alfred Moore, of Brunswick, a soldier of the Revolution and afterwards a Justice of the Supreme Court of the United States The county seat is Carthage.

Nash—Nash County was formed in 1777 from Edgecombe, was

named in honor of General Francis Nash, a soldier of the Revolution, who was mortally wounded while fighting under Washington at Germantown. The United States has erected a monument in his honor at the Guilford Battle Ground near Greensboro. The county seat is Nashville.

New Hanover.—New Hanover County was formed in 1729 from Bath, was named after Hanover, a country in Europe whose ruler became King of England, with the title of George I. The county seat is Wilmington.

Northampton.—Northampton County was formed in 1741 from Bertie, was named in honor of George, Earl of Northampton, an English Nobleman. His son, Spencer Compton, Earl of Wilmington, was high in office when Gabriel Johnston was Governor of North Carolina, who had the town of Wilmington named in his honor. The county seat is Jackson.

Onslow —Onslow County was formed in 1734 from Bath, was named in honor of Arthur Onslow, for more than thirty years speaker of the House of Commons in the British Parliament. The county seat is Jacksonville.

Orange.—Orange County was formed in 1753 from Granville, Johnston, and Bladen, was named in honor of William of Orange, who became King William III of England He was one of the greatest of the kings of England and saved the English people from the tyranny of James II. His name is held in honor wherever English liberty is enjoyed. The county seat is Hillsboro.

Pamlico —Pamlico County was formed in 1872 from Craven and Beaufort, was named after the sound of the same name, which was the name of a tribe of Indians in Eastern North Carolina. There was a Pamlico precinct in North Carolina as early as 1705. Pamlico County voted with Beaufort up to 1883. The county seat is Bayboro

Pasquotank —Pasquotank County was formed in 1672 from Albemarle, was named for a tribe of Indians in Eastern part of State The county seat is Elizabeth City

Pender —Pender County was formed in 1875 from New Hanover, was named in honor of General William D Pender, of Edgecombe County, a brave Confederate soldier who was killed at the battle of Gettysburg. The last order given by the famous Stonewall Jackson on the battle field was to General Pender· "You must hold your ground, General Pender, you must hold your ground." he cried as he was carried off the field to die. General Pender held his ground The county seat is Burgaw.

Perquimans—Perquimans was formed in 1672 from Albemarle, was named after a tribe of Indians. The county seat is Hertford

Person —Person County was formed in 1791 from Caswell, was named in honor of General Thomas Person, Revolutionary patriot, member of the Council of Safety, and Trustee of the University. He gave a large sum of money to the University, and a building was erected in his honor called Person Hall. The county seat is Roxboro

Pitt —Pitt County was formed in 1760 from Beaufort, was named in honor of William Pitt (see Chatham County) The county seat is Greenville.

Polk —Polk County was formed in 1855 from Rutherford and Henderson, was named in honor of Col William Polk who rendered distinguished service in the battles of Germantown, Brandywine. and Eutaw in all of which he was wounded. The county seat is Columbus. Polk County voted with Rutherford until 1868.

Randolph.—Randolph County was formed in 1779 from Guilford, was named in honor of Peyton Randolph, of Virginia. the President of the First Continental Congress. The county seat is Ashboro

Richmond —Richmond County was formed in 1779 from Anson, was named in honor of Charles Lennox. Duke of Richmond. Principal Secretary He was a strong friend of the American colonies and made the motion in the House of Lords that they be granted their independence. The county seat is Rockingham.

Robeson.—Robeson County was formed in 1786 from Bladen, was named in honor of Col Thomas Robeson, a soldier of the Revolution He was one of the leaders of the battle of Elizabethton, which was fought in September, 1781. By this battle the Tories in the Southeastern part of the State were crushed forever. The commander of the Whigs was Col Thomas Brown The county seat is Lumberton

Rockingham.—Rockingham County was formed in 1785 from Guilford, was named in honor of Charles Watson Wentworth, Marquis of Rockingham, who was the leader of the party in the British Parliament that advocated American independence. He ws Prime Minister when the Stamp Act was repealed. The county seat is Wentworth

Rowan.—Rowan County was formed in 1753 from Anson, was named in honor of Matthew Rowan, a prominent leader before the Revolution and for a short time after the death of Gov. Gabriel Johnston, acting Gov. The county seat is Salisbury.

Rutherford —Rutherford County was formed in 1779 from Tryon and Burke, was named in honor of General Griffith Rutherford, one of the most prominent of the Revolutionary patriots. He led the expedition that crushed the Cherokees in 1776 and rendered other important services, both in the Legislature and on the battle field. The county seat is Rutherfordton.

Sampson.—Sampson County was formed in 1784 from Duplin and New Hanover, was named in honor of Colonel Sampson, who was a member of Gov Martin's council. The county seat is Clinton.

Scotland.—Scotland County was formed in 1899 from Richmond was named after the country of Scotland, the northern part of the island of Great Britain Most of the people in this county are descendants of Scotch Highlanders The county seat is Laurinburg.

OLD FLAX WHEEL. (SEE PAGE 26)

Stanly—Stanly County was formed in 1841 from Montgomery, was named in honor of John Stanly, for many years a member of the Legislature and several times speaker of the House of Commons The county seat is Albemarle.

Stokes—Stokes County was formed in 1798 from Surry, was named in honor of Col. John Stokes, a brave soldier in the Revolution who was desperately wounded at the Waxhaw Massacre when Col. Buford's regiment was cut to pieces by Tarleton. After the war Washington appointed him judge of the United States Court in North Carolina The county seat is Danbury.

Surry—Surry County was formed in 1770 from Rowan, was named in honor of Lord Surry, a prominent member of Parliament who opposed the taxation of the American colonies by Parliament The county seat is Rockford.

Swain.—Swain County was formed in 1871 from Jackson and Macon, was named in honor of David Lowrie Swain, Governor of North Carolina and President of the University. The county seat is Bryson City.

Transylvania—Transylvania County was formed in 1861 from Henderson and Jackson, the name is derived from two Latin words, "trans" across and "sylva," woods The county seat is Brevard. Transylvania County voted with Henderson until 1868.

Tryon—Tryon County was formed in 1769 in honor of Gov. William Tryon, who was twice Governor of North Carolina. It was abolished in 1779

The first county seat of Tryon County was on Main Broad River, just above Ellis' Ferry, and was laid off in 1769. The county seat was in a beautiful place, a natural eminence with an abundance of springs of pure cold water, and about one-half mile above Ellis' Ferry. At that time Broad River was navigated up to the county seat, there being no less than two flat-bottomed boats regularly plying up and down the river The boats continued until the Revolutionary war and traffic was never resumed by boat afterward

5

Parenthetically, I remind that the first General Assembly ever held in North Carolina—so authentic history states—was in Pasquotank County, North Carolina, near Nixonton, under a giant oak tree, on the left hand side of the road. It is interesting to note that one of the by-laws of that Assembly admonished that "all members should wear shoes, if not stockings, during the sessions of the body, and they must refrain from throwing chicken and other bones under the tree." We would that we were given time to speculate on the deliberations of that early body, suffice it to say, however, that the inspiration of the giant oak and the freedom of the expansive open must have suggested to the pioneer legislators the sturdiness and freedom of government given us today. The little "acorn" legislature held there in that distant day has grown into the great law-tree of today

Tyrrell.—Tyrrell County was formed in 1729 from Albemarle, was named in honor of Sir John Tyrrell, who at one time was one of the Lord Proprietors. The county seat is Columbia

Union—Union County was formed in 1842 from Anson and Mecklenburg. The county seat is Monroe.

Vance—Vance County was formed in 1881 from Granville, Warren, and Franklin, was named in honor of Zebulon B. Vance, the great war Governor, a member of Congress, Governor of North Carolina, United States Senator. County seat Henderson.

Wake—Wake County was formed in 1770 from Johnston, Cumberland, and Orange, was named in honor of Gov. Tryon's wife, whose maiden name was Margaret Wake. Some historians say that the county was named for Esther Wake, the popular sister of Tryon's wife, but there is no reason to suppose that any such person ever existed. She is purely a creature of the imagination. The county seat is Raleigh.

Warren.—Warren County was formed in 1779 from Bute, was named in honor of General Joseph Warren, a brave Massachusetts soldier who fell while fighting at the Battle of Bunker Hill. The county se   W

Washington —Washington County was formed in 1799 from Tyrrell, was named in honor of George Washington. The county seat is Plymouth.

Watauga.—Watauga County was formed in 1849 from Ashe, Wilkes, Caldwell and Yancy, was named after an Indian tribe. The county seat is Boone.

Wayne —Wayne County was formed in 1779 from Dobbs and Craven, was named in honor of General Anthony Wayne, one of Washington's most trusted soldiers. His courage was so great as to almost amount to rashness and his soldiers called him "Mad Anthony Wayne." The county seat is Goldsboro.

Wilkes —Wilkes County was formed in 1777 from Surry and Burke was named in honor of John Wilkes Wilkes was a violent opponent of the Tory party in England, which would not let him take his seat in Parliament, to which he had been elected. The Americans imagined that he was suffering in the cause of liberty and named the county in his honor The county seat is Wilkesboro

Wilson.—Wilson County was formed in 1855 from Edgecombe, Nash, Johnston, and Wayne, was named in honor of Louis E Wilson, many times a member of the Legislature from Edgecombe County, a soldier of the Mexican War, who died near Vera Cruz of fever He was a benefactor of the poor of the native county. The county seat is Wilson From 1856 to 1868 Wilson voted with Edgecombe.

Yadkin —-Yadkin County was formed in 1850 from Surry. Its name is derived from the Yadkin River, which runs through it It is supposed to be an Indian name The county seat is Yadkinville. Yadkin voted with Surry in 1852

Yancey.—Yancey County was formed in 1833 from Burke and Buncombe, was named in honor of Bartlett Yancey, an eloquent orator, many times a member of the Legislature, speaker of the State Senate and a member of Congress He was one of the earliest advocates of the public school system of North Carolina. The county seat is Burnsville.

DATA OF STATES AND TERRITORIES

State or Territory	Square Miles	Admitted to Union	Settled	Capital	Nickname of State	Nickname of People
Alabama	52,250	Dec 11, 1819	1702	Montgomery	Cotton	Lizards
Alaska	590,884	July 27, 1868	1801	Sitka		
Arizona	113,020	Feb 24, 1863	1580	Phoenix		
Arkansas	53,850	June 15, 1836	1685	Little Rock	Bear	Toothpicks
California	158,360	Sept 9, 1850	1769	Sacramento	Golden	Gold Hunters
Colorado	103,925	Aug 1, 1876	1858	Denver	Centennial	Rovers
Connecticut	4,990	Jan 9, 1788	1635	Hartford	Nutmeg	Wooden Nutmegs
Delaware	2,050	Dec 7, 1787	1627	Dover	Blue Hen	Blue Hens, Chickens
District of Columbia	70	July 16, 1790	1660	Washington		
Florida	58,680	March 3, 1845	1565	Tallahassee	Peninsula, Flower	Fly-up-the-Creeks
Georgia	59,475	Jan 2, 1788	1733	Atlanta	Cracker	Crackers
Guam	1,250	Aug 12, 1898	1667	Agana		
Hawaii	6,740	April 30, 1900	1778	Honolulu		Kanakas
Idaho	84,800	July 3, 1890	1842	Boise City		
Illinois	56,650	Dec 3, 1818	1720	Springfield	Prairie	Suckers
Indiana	36,350	Dec 11, 1816	1730	Indianapolis	Hoosier	Hoosiers
Iowa	56,025	March 3, 1845	1788	Des Moines	Hawkeye	Hawkeye
Kansas	82,080	Jan 29, 1861	1831	Topeka	Sunflower	Jayhawkers
Kentucky	40,400	Feb 4, 1792	1765	Frankfort	Blue Grass	Corncrackers
Louisiana	48,720	April 8, 1812	1699	Baton Rouge	Pelican	Creoles
Maine	33,040	March 3, 1820	1624	Augusta	Pine Tree	Foxes
Maryland	12,210	April 28, 1788	1634	Annapolis	Old Line	Crowthumpers
Massachusetts	8,315	Feb 6, 1788	1620	Boston	Bay	Beaneaters
Michigan	58,915	Jan 26, 1837	1650	Lansing	Wolverine	Wolverines
Minnesota	83,365	May 11, 1858	1805	St Paul	Gopher, North Star	Gophers
Mississippi	46,810	Dec 10, 1817	1716	Jackson	Bayou	Tadpoles
Missouri	69,415	March 2, 1821	1764	Jefferson City	Show Me	Pukes
Montana	146,080	Nov 1, 1889	1809	Helena	Stub Toe	
Nebraska	77,510	March 1, 1867	1817	Lincoln		Bugeaters
Nevada	110,700	Oct 13, 1864	1850	Carson City	Silver	Sage Hens
New Hampshire	9,305	June 21, 1788	1623	Concord	Granite	Granite Boys

State	Population	Date	Settled	Capital	Blue	Jersey Blues
New Jersey	7,815	Dec 18, 1787	1620	Trenton	Blue	Jersey Blues
New Mexico	122,580	Sept 9, 1850	1537	Santa Fe		
New York	19,170	July 26, 1788	1611	Albany	Empire	Knickerbockers
North Carolina	52,250	Nov 21, 1789	1650	Raleigh	Old North	Tarheels
North Dakota	70,795	Nov 2, 1889	1780	Bismarck	Sioux	Tuckoes
Ohio	41,060	Nov 29, 1802	1788	Columbus	Buckeye	Buckeyes
Oklahoma	70,130	Nov 16, 1907	1889	Guthrie		
Oregon	96,030	Feb 11, 1859	1810	Salem	Beaver	Webfeet
Pennsylvania	45,215	Dec 12, 1787	1682	Harrisburg	Keystone	Leatherheads
Philippines	140,000	Nov 28, 1898	1565	Manila		Filipinos
Porto Rico	3,600	Aug 12, 1898	1510	San Juan		
Rhode Island	1,250	May 29, 1790	1636	Providence	Little Rhody	Gun Flints
South Carolina	30,570	May 23, 1788	1670	Columbia	Palmetto	Weasles
South Dakota	77,650	Nov 2, 1889	1856	Pierre	Coyote	Singed Cats
Tennessee	42,050	June 1, 1796	1757	Nashville	Volunteer	Butternuts
Texas	265,780	Dec 29, 1845	1686	Austin	Lone Star	Beetheads
Utah	81,970	Jan 4, 1896	1847	Salt Lake City		
Vermont	9,565	Feb 18, 1791	1761	Montpelier	Green Mountain	Green Mt Boys
Virginia	12,150	June 26, 1788	1607	Richmond	Old Dominion	Beadles
Washington	69,180	Nov 11, 1889	1811	Olympia	Chinook	Chinooks
West Virginia	21,780	Dec 31, 1862	1774	Charleston	Panhandle	Panhandlers
Wisconsin	56,040	May 29, 1848	1670	Madison	Badger	Badgers
Wyoming	97,890	July 11, 1890	1834	Cheyenne		

GOVERNORS UNDER THE CROWN

Richard Everard	May, 1728–Feb. 25th, 1731	Arthur Dobbs	Nov 2nd, 1751–March 28th, 1765
George Burrington	Feb 15th, 1731–April 15th, 1734	William Tryon	March 28th, 1765–Dec 20th, 1765
Samuel Rice	April 13th, 1734–Oct 27th, 1734	William Tryon	Dec 20th, 1765–July 1st, 1771
Gabriel Johnston	Oct 27th, 1734–July 17th, 1752	James Hasell	July 1st, 1771–Aug 12th, 1771
Matthew Rowan	July 17th, 1752–Nov. 2nd, 1754	Josiah Martin	Aug 12th, 1771–May 17th, 1775

GOVERNORS OF NORTH CAROLINA SINCE INDEPENDENCE

ELECTED BY THE LEGISLATURE

Richard Caswell	Lenoir County	Dec 19th, 1776–April 18th, 1777
Richard Caswell	Lenoir County	April 18th, 1777–April 18th, 1778
Richard Caswell	Lenoir County	April 18th, 1778–May 4th, 1779
Richard Caswell	Lenoir County	May 4th, 1779–April 1780
Abner Nash	Craven County	April 1780–June 26th, 1781
Thomas Burke	Orange County	June 26th, 1781–April 26th, 1782
Alexander Martin	Guilford County	April 26th, 1782–April 30th, 1783
Alexander Martin	Guilford County	April 30th, 1783–April 30th, 1785
Richard Caswell	Lenoir County	April 1785–Dec 12th, 1785
Richard Caswell	Lenoir County	Dec 12th, 1785–Dec. 23rd, 1786
Richard Caswell	Lenoir County	Dec. 23rd, 1786–Dec 20th, 1787

Samuel Johnston	Chowan County	Dec 20th, 1787–Nov. 18th, 1788
Samuel Johnston	Chowan County	Nov 18th, 1788–Nov 16th, 1789
Samuel Johnston	Chowan County	Nov. 16th, 1789–Dec. 17th, 1789
Alexander Martin	Guilford County	Dec 17th, 1789–Dec 9th, 1790
Alexander Martin	Guilford County	Dec 9th, 1790–Jan 2nd, 1792
Alexander Martin	Guilford County	Jan. 2nd, 1792–Dec 14th, 1792
R D Spaight	Craven County	Dec 14th, 1792–Dec. 26th, 1793
R D Spaight	Craven County	Dec 26th, 1793–Jan 6th, 1795
R D Spaight	Craven County	Jan. 6th, 1795–Nov 19th, 1795
Samuel Ashe	New Hanover County	Nov 19th, 1795–Dec. 19th, 1796
Samuel Ashe	New Hanover County	Dec 19th, 1796–Dec 5th, 1797
Samuel Ashe	New Hanover County	Dec 5th, 1797–Dec 7th, 1798
W R Davie	Halifax County	Dec 7th, 1798–Nov 23rd, 1799
Benjamin Williams	Moore County	Nov. 23d, 1799–Nov 29th, 1800
Benjamin Williams	Moore County	Nov. 29th, 1800–Nov 28th, 1801
Benjamin Williams	Moore County	Nov 28th, 1801–Dec 6th, 1802
James Turner	Warren County	Dec 6th, 1802–Dec. 1st, 1803
James Turner	Warren County	Dec 1st, 1803–Nov 29th, 1804
James Turner	Warren County	Nov 29th, 1804–Dec 10th, 1805
Nathaniel Alexander	Mecklenburg County	Dec. 10th, 1805–Dec 1st, 1806
Nathaniel Alexander	Mecklenburg County	Dec 1st, 1806–Dec 1st, 1807
Benjamin Williams	Moore County	Dec 7th, 1807–Dec 12th, 1808
David Stone	Bertie County	Dec 12th, 1808–Dec 13th, 1809
David Stone	Bertie County	Dec 13th, 1809–Dec 5th, 1810
Benjamin Smith	Brunswick County	Dec 5th, 1810–Dec 9th, 1811
William Hawkins	Warren County	Dec 9th 1811–Nov 25th, 1812

GOVERNORS OF NORTH CAROLINA SINCE INDEPENDENCE—CONTINUED

ELECTED BY THE LEGISLATURE—CONTINUED

m Hawkins	Warren County	Nov 29th, 1812–Nov 20th, 1813
m Hawkins	Warren County	Nov 20th, 1813–Nov 29th, 1814
m Miller	Warren County	Nov 29th, 1814–Dec 7th, 1815
m Miller	Warren County	Dec 7th, 1815 Dec 7th, 1816
m Miller	Warren County	Dec 7th, 1816–Dec 3rd, 1817
Branch	Halifax County	Dec 3rd, 1817–Nov 20th, 1818
Branch	Halifax County	Nov 20th, 1818–Nov 25th, 1819
Branch	Halifax County	Nov 25th, 1819–Dec 7th, 1820
Franklin	Surry County	Dec 7th, 1820–Dec 7th, 1821
el Holmes	Sampson County	Dec 7th, 1821–Dec 7th, 1822
el Holmes	Sampson County	Dec 7th 1822–Dec 6th, 1823
el Holmes	Sampson County	Dec 6th, 1823–Dec 7th, 1824
Burton	Halifax County	Dec 7th, 1824–Dec 6th, 1825
Burton	Halifax County	Dec 6th, 1825–Dec 29th, 1826
Burton	Halifax County	Dec 29th, 1826–Dec 8th, 1827
s Iredell	Chowan County	Dec 8th, 1827 Dec 12th, 1828
John Owen	Bladen County	Dec 12th, 1828–Dec 10th, 1829
John Owen	Bladen County	Dec 10th 1829–Dec 18th, 1830
Montfort Stokes	Wilkes County	Dec 18th, 1830–Dec 13th, 1831

Montfort Stokes	Wilkes County	Dec 13th, 1831–Dec 6th, 1832
L. D Swain	Buncombe County	Dec 6th, 1832–Dec 9th, 1833
D Swain	Buncombe County	Dec 9th, 1833–Dec 10th, 1834
D Swain	Buncombe County	Dec 10th, 1834–Dec 10th, 1835
D Speight, Jr	Craven County	Dec 10th, 1835–Dec 31st, 1836

GOVERNORS OF NORTH CAROLINA SINCE INDEPENDENCE—Continued

GOVERNORS ELECTED BY THE PEOPLE

E. B. Dudley	New Hanover County	Dec. 31st, 1836–Dec 29th, 1838
E. B. Dudley	New Hanover County	Dec 29th, 1838–Jan 1st, 1841
J. M. Morehead	Guilford County	Jan 1st, 1841–Dec 31st, 1842
J. M. Morehead	Guilford County	Dec 31st, 1842–Jan 1st, 1845
W. A. Graham	Orange County	Jan 1st, 1845–Jan 1st, 1817
W. A. Graham	Orange County	Jan 1st, 1817–Jan. 1st, 1849
C. Manly	Wake County	Jan 1st, 1849–Jan 1st, 1851
D. S. Reid	Rockingham County	Jan 1st, 1851–Dec 2nd, 1852
D. S. Reid	Rockingham County	Dec 22nd, 1852–Dec 6th, 1854
Warren Winslow	Cumberland County	Dec 6th, 1854–Jan 1st, 1855
Thomas Bragg	Northampton County	Jan 1st, 1855–Jan. 1st, 1857
Thomas Bragg	Northampton County	Jan 1st, 1857–Jan. 1st, 1859
John W. Ellis	Rowan County	Jan 1st, 1859–Jan 1st, 1861
John W. Ellis	Rowan County	Jan 1st, 1861–July 7th, 1861
Henry T Clark	Edgecombe County	July 7th, 1861–Sept. 8th, 1862
Z. B. Vance	Buncombe County	Sept 8th, 1862–Dec 22nd, 1864
Z. B. Vance	Buncombe County	Dec 22nd, 1864–May 29th, 1865
W. W. Holden	Wake County	May 29th, 1865–Dec. 15th, 1865
Jonathan Worth	Randolph County	Dec 15th, 1865–Dec 22nd, 1866
Jonathan Worth	Randolph County	Dec. 22nd, 1866–July 1st, 1868
W. W. Holden*	Wake County	July 1st, 1868–Dec 5th, 1870
T. R. Caldwell	Burke County	Dec 15th, 1870–Jan 1st, 1873

T R Caldwell	Burke County	Jan 1st, 1873–July	7th, 1871
C H Brogden	Wayne County	July 11th 1871–Jan	1st, 1877
Z B Vance	Mecklenburg County	Jan 1st, 1877–Feb	5th, 1879
T J Jarvis	Pitt County	Feb. 5th, 1879–Jan.	18th, 1881
T J Jarvis	Pitt County	Jan 18th, 1881–Jan	21st, 1885
A M Scales	Rockingham County	Jan 1st, 1885–Jan	17th, 1889
D G Fowle	Wake County	Jan 17th, 1889–April	8th, 1891
Thomas M Holt	Alamance County	April 8th, 1891–Jan	18th, 1893
Thus Carr	Edgecombe County	Jan 18th, 1893–Jan	12th, 1897
D L Russell	Brunswick County	Jan 12th, 1897–Jan	15th, 1901
C B Aycock	Wayne County	Jan 15th, 1901–Jan.	11th, 1905
R B Glenn	Forsyth County	Jan 11th, 1905–Jan	12th, 1909
W W Kitchin	Person County	Jan 12th, 1909–Jan	15th, 1913
Locke Craig	Buncombe County	Jan 15th, 1913–Jan	15th, 1917
Thomas W Bickett	Franklin County	Jan 15th, 1917–Jan	15th, 1921

*W W Holden was impeached and removed from office in 1870 For the first time in the history of the State of North Carolina, the High Court of Impeachment was organized for the purpose of impeaching the Governor The accusations against the Governor were 'high crimes and misdemeanors" The result of the trial was conviction and the removal of the Governor from office

CHAPTER 1 *First Generation*

George Hamrick from Germany in 1731   Married Nancy Cook.

CHAPTER 2. *Second Generation*

Children of George Hamrick and wife, Nancy Cook   George married Susanna Blanton   Benjamin married Fannie Burchett. Moses Richard married Mary Bridges

CHAPTER 3 *Third Generation.*

Children of George Hamrick and wife Susanna Blanton· Samuel married Mary Hamrick. James Married Susannah Hamrick   Jones never married   Frederick never married. Rebecca married James Bridges   Susanna married William McSwain   Mollie married William Champion

CHAPTER 4. *Fourth Generation.*

Children of Samuel Hamrick and wife, Mary Hamrick. James married Frankie Blanton   Elijah married Mary McSwain; second wife Margaret McSwain   John married Barbara Maruney   Reuben married Hannah McSwain. David married Rebecca Raney, second wife, Sarah McSwain   Samuel married Susanna Adams   Nancy married Hezekiah Wilkins   Elizabeth married James Bridges   Mollie married Samuel Bridges. Susanna married David McSwain

CHAPTER 5 *Fifth Generation.*

Children of James Hamrick and wife, Frankie Blanton: William married Hannah Randall, second wife, Jane McEntire   Albert married Martha Hicks   Allen married Susanna McSwain; second wife, Elizabeth Nolan   Thompson married Essie Stone, second wife, Essie Runyans

CHAPTER 6 *Sixth Generation.*

Children of William Hamrick and wife Hannah Randall· Thomas married I
                                          Caswell

married Milhe McEntire   Jacob married Nancy Idlet.   Sarah married Oliver P. Gibson   Elizabeth married George Blanton.   Narcissus married Anthony Dickey.   Adolphus never married.   Drury Dobbins never married.

Children of William Hamrick and wife, Jane McEntire: Drayton married Margaret Camp.   Jane married Monroe Moore   Philo never married.   Two infants.

CHAPTER 7. *Seventh Generation.*

Children of Thomas Hamrick and wife, Rebecca Marks: William S married Mary Roberts.   Thomas Wells married Pauline Marks. Franklin married Louisa Green   Hudson married Lenora Hartgrove Sarah Evelyn married Thomas Button.   Lilly married Marion Button   Eulas never married   John never married.   Charles never married   Jesse not married.

CHAPTER 8 *Seventh Generation.*

Children of Rufus Hamrick and wife, Louisa Blanton.   Eli married Charleey Wiley.   Thompson married Ida Humphries   William married Saleny Champion.   Delphus married Charlotte Cleary Giles L married Docia Camp.   Susanna married James Crawford. John married Martha Beheeler..   Jacob married Carrie Smith.

CHAPTER 9. *Seventh Generation*

Children of Caswell Hamrick and wife, Milhe McEntie: Ackellie married Mollie Smith.   Wiley married Mary Starnes, second wife, Vernie Putnam.   George married Callie Moore   Coleman never married.

CHAPTER 10. *Seventh Generation.*

Children of Jacob Hamrick and wife Nancy Idlet·   Roswell never married.

CHAPTER 11. *Seventh Generation.*

Children of Oliver P. Gipson and wife Sarah Hamrick·   Syrus married Ida Stephens   Victoria married Joseph Mullinaux   Mary married Daniel Turner   Alice never married   Sarah not married.

CHAPTER 12. *Seventh Generation.*

Children of George Blanton and wife, Elizabeth Hamrick. Elzeberry married Ruth Wright.   Ruphus married Mattie Williams Julius married Susanna Williams.   Thomas married Ollie Holland. Louis married Ella Costner.   Enoch married Laura Ward.   Lowe married Sarah Fisher   Carrie married Nathaniel Miller; second wife, Etta Brown   Harriet married Eli Rich   Xenophan married ———— Hull.

CHAPTER 13. *Seventh Generation*

Children of Anthony Dickey and wife, Narcissus Hamrick: Elvira married James Moore. Mary married Monroe Moore   Texanna married John Turner   Laura married Clarence Hunter.   William Anthony never married.

CHAPTER 14 *Seventh Generation.*

Children of Drayton Hamrick and wife, Margaret Camp   Joseph married Loy Taylor   Carrie married Grayson Osteen. Julia never married. Clara never married.

CHAPTER 15. *Seventh Generation*

Children of Monroe Moore and wife, Jane Hamrick· Elizabeth married James Bright   Hattie Jane married Effort Jones. Francis Marion married Fannie Elliott. Alice O'Neil married Jarome Martin.

Children of Monroe Moore and wife, Mary Dickey. Anthony never married. Clarence Victor never married   Marvin Eula never married   Siddie not married.

CHAPTER 16 *Sixth Generation*

Childre   . . . . H . . . . Martha Hick-   Miles married Sarah Ann Hopper. Dillie married James Weir. Calvin married Cordelia Hicks. Elizabeth married Lumpkin Wiley.

CHAPTER 17. *Seventh Generation.*

Children of Miles Hamrick and wife, Sarah Ann Hopper. Calvin married Margaret Ross Hudson married Mary Gardner. Fannie married William Poston. Julia married George Hunt. Martha never married. Carrie never married. Lenore never married Clifton never married. Albert never married.

CHAPTER 18. *Seventh Generation.*

Children of Calvin Hamrick and wife, Cordelia Hicks Calvin never married.

CHAPTER 19. *Seventh Generation*

Children of Lumpkin Wiley and wife, Elizabeth Hamrick· Cyrus never married. One infant.

CHAPTER 20. *Seventh Generation.*

Children of James Weir and wife, Dillie Hamrick· John Albert married Addie Houston. Martha Elizabeth married Joseph W. Bridges. Newman married Mary Huffstettler. William J. married Virginia Susanna Beam. Milas married Georgie Neal Margaret married George Barber. Robert never married. Wheeler never married.

CHAPTER 21 *Sixth Generation.*

Children of Allen Hamrick and wife, Susanna McSwain· Elphus married Lucinda Carpenter, second wife, Elizabeth Stroup, third wife. Roxanna Jones. Thompson married Martha Grigg; second wife, Georgianna Grigg. Dillard married Matilda Gardner. Jane married Phillip Wright Hannah married Monroe McSwain. Susanna married George Collins Albert never married. Margaret never married Hester never married.

CHAPTER 22. *Seventh Generation.*

Children of Elphus Hamrick and wife, Lucinda Carpenter. Albert married Amanda Hendrick. Cleophus married Sarah Hoyle Mary married Wade Williamson Susanna married Barnett McSwain Vianna married William Grigg. Alphonso married ———.

Children of Elphus Hamrick and wife Elizabeth Stroup Vader married Henry Cabiness.

CHAPTER 23 *Seventh Generation*

Children of Dillard Hamrick and wife, Matilda Gardner. Edgar married Olive Gardner. Julia married Bylus F. Gardner. Docia married John H. Lackey Florence married Preston Costner. Della married Grady Wilson. William S married Emma Cline. Lemuel married Edith Smith Clifton never married. Mary Jane never married Vangie married Grady Smith. Ruby not married. Bivie not married.

CHAPTER 24. *Sixth Generation.*

Children of Thompson Hamrick and wife, Essie Stone: William Andrew married Cordelia Hicks John ———. Harvey ———

CHAPTER 25. *Seventh Generation*

Children of William Andrew and wife. Cordelia Hicks. Mary Etta married Richard Anthony Essie never married.

CHAPTER 26. *Seventh Generation*

Children of Thompson Hamrick and wife, Martha Grigg Cleary married Joshua Wright. Minnie never married. Jasper never married

Children of Thompson Hamrick and wife, Georgianna Grigg: Benna not married. Loyd not married Posey not married. Dimsey not married

CHAPTER 27. *Seventh Generation.*

Child   t'   , W   d   la Hamrick   David

married Pantha Hamrick.   Jane married Clifton McSwain   Thomas married Elizabeth Beam   Susanna married Sylvannus Grigg   Ellen married Albert Scism   Hannah Margaret married William Williams.

Chapter 28 *Seventh Generation*

Children of Monroe McSwain and wife, Hannah Hamrick. Nancy married Monroe Wright   Effie never married. Henry not married. Julia not married. Maggie not married   Eva not married. Allen not married.

Chapter 29 *Fifth Generation*

Children of Elijah Hamrick and wife, Mary McSwain. William married Jane McSwain. Samuel married Penina McSwain   David married Sarah Hamrick.   James married Mary McSwain. Elijah married Hannah Hamrick   Mary married George McSwain, second husband, John McSwain. Judith married William McSwain   Elizabeth married David McSwain   One infant

Children of Elijah Hamrick and wife, Margaret McSwain. George Robinson married Rebecca Hamrick; second wife, Sarah Matheney, third wife, Elvira Hamrick.   Johnothan McSwain married Elizabeth Hamrick   Catherine married Berry Hamrick   Nancy married John Judson Jones   Reuben married Jane Pinson, second wife, Phoebia Hamrick. Sarah married Charles Jefferson Hamrick. Jane married Drury Harrell   John never married   Rebecca never married.

Chapter 30. *Sixth Generation.*

Children of William Hamrick and wife, Jane McSwain· Elijah married Catherine Bridges   James married Susanna Wright Samuel married Lettie Durham   David married Caroline Hardin   Drury Dobbins married Sara Hardin   Doctor Abram F. married Susanna Jones   Thomas never married

Chapter 31. *Seventh Generation.*

Children of Elijah Hamrick and wife, Catherine Bridges. Samuel married Alice Blanton   Doctor married Nancy Blanton   Caleb

6

married Viola Robbins   Amanda married Elijah Webb, second husband, Perry Humphries. Docia married Perry Holland. Ollie married Demus Blanton. Patience not married.

CHAPTER 32. *Seventh Generation.*

Children of James Hamrick and wife, Susanna Wright: Carva married Priscilla Owens   Alonzo Oliver married Ollie Green   Lucındy married William Burns   Patience married Edmond L Jenkins   Victoria married Joseph Wilson   Callie married Jesse Owen; second husband, Martin Hunnicutt. Mollie married Crayton Green, second husband, Martin Hunnicutt   Johnnie married Luther Hamrick. Sumetress married Clayton Wiggins

CHAPTER 33. *Seventh Generation.*

Children of Drury Dobbins Hamrick and wife, Sarah Hardin· Clementine married Francis Newman Gardner.

CHAPTER 34 *Seventh Generation*

Children of David Hamrick and wife. Caroline Hardin   Jane married Jesse Whitston Bridges   Hessentine married James Franklin Bridges.

CHAPTER 35. *Seventh Generation*

Children of Doctor Abram F. Hamrick and wife, Susanna Jones· Laura married J. P. D. Withrow. Blanch married Theodoro Heafner   Carrie married William Thomas Calton

CHAPTER 36 *Seventh Generation*

Children of Samuel Hamrick and wife. Penınah McSwaın. William Aseph married Louisa Jane Borders   James Madison married Frances Grubbs   Samuel married Margaret Glover   David Jones married Aveline Rodgers   John never married   Sarah never married

Chapter 37. *Seventh Generation*

Children of Samuel Hamrick and wife, Lettie Durham· Clinton
———— ———— ————. Exenophan ———— ———— ————. Missouri ———— ————
————.

Chapter 38. *Seventh Generation.*

Children of William Aseph Hamrick and wife Louisa Jane Bor-
ders: John Leon married Susanna Hawks, second wife, Bessie
McEntire. Alfred married Alice Hartsfield. Jesse W. married
Hattie Lightsey. Jane married Adam Hartsfield Susanna married
Joseph Walker Walter married Ruth Hawks. Mary married ————
Letworth. Sarah Jane married Perry Boseymon.

Chapter 39. *Seventh Generation.*

Children of James Madison Hamrick and wife, Frances Grubbs.
Lela married Thomas McClellan. Rebecca married Ruphus Mc-
Clellan. Jane married Lawrence McClellan. Franklin married
Lillie Sledge Charles not married Emma not married Sadie
not married

Chapter 40 *Seventh Generation*

Children of Samuel Hamrick and wife, Margaret Glover. Susanna married Lee Mills. Lillie married ———— Luddington, second
husband, Jesse Breedlove. Willie ———— ———— ———— Mollie married
———— Glidwell. Jesse married ———— Johnson. Henry
———— ———— ———— John ———— ———— ———— Lee ———— ———— —

Chapter 41. *Seventh Generation*

Children of David Jones Hamrick and wife, Angeline Rodgers·
Minnie married Avie Henderson Edgie married Mitchell Henderson Burwell married Clara Ward Doctor Oliver married Maudie
Bishop. Ada married Stover Walker Benjamin married Susanna
Turner Thomas never married Ellen never married. Letitia
never married. Doctor Bascomb never married. Turner never
married Nellie never married. Lawyer never married Ellis not
married.

CHAPTER 42   *Sixth Generation.*

Children of David Hamrick and wife, Sarah Hamrick. Perry married Roxanna Hamrick. Hannah married George McSwain; second husband, James Hawkins. Judith married Joseph Price. Martha never married

CHAPTER 43   *Seventh Generation*

Children of Perry Hamrick and wife, Roxanna Hamrick· Permelia married Madison Brooks. Docia married Preston Hawkins

CHAPTER 44   *Seventh Generation*

Children of Joseph Price and wife, Judith Hamrick: Mary married Hamrick McSwain

CHAPTER 45   *Sixth Generation.*

Children of James Hamrick and wife, Mary McSwain· William married Sylvira Ledbetter. second wife, Sarah Champion. Elijah married Elizabeth McSwain. Joseph married Lucretia Jolley. Isaac married Silveraney Jolley. Abram married Nancy McSwain. James Louis married Sarah McSwain. Thomas married Elmina Matheney; second wife, Margaret McSwain. Julia Ann married Thomas Lovelace. Mary Jane married George Champion. Sarah married George Champion. Rebecca married Thomas McSwain. Louisa married William Harrell; second husband, Perry Lovelace (no children). Susanna married Gilead Green. Emiline married Ambrose McSwain. Roxanna married Perry Hamrick. David never married. Five infants.

CHAPTER 46   *Seventh Generation*

Children of Elijah Hamrick and wife, Elizabeth McSwain: Samuel married Vianna Padgett. Mary married John Stewart.

CHAPTER 47   *Seventh Generation*

Childr   H   Joanna

married Austin Turner Mary Elizabeth never married. Charles never married

CHAPTER 48. *Seventh Generation.*

Children of Isaac Hamrick and wife, Silveraney Jolley. James Thomas married Julia Blanton One infant.

CHAPTER 49. *Seventh Generation.*

Children of Abram Hamrick and wife Nancy McSwain· Oliver Abram married Julia Blanton James Louis married Sarah Blanton Martha married John Blanton, second husband, William Jasper Jones. Julia married James Withrow. Elijah married Alda Putnam. Roxanna married Elam McKinney Hannah married Chivus Gettys Eva married George Putnam. Pinkney never married. Mary never married.

CHAPTER 50. *Seventh Generation.*

Children of Thomas McSwain and wife, Rebecca Hamrick Alice married David Richard McSwain Henry married Nancy Neal Blanch never married

CHAPTER 51. *Seventh Generation.*

Children of Thomas Hamrick and wife, Elmina Matheney John married Ella Stockton. Panthia married David Wright James never married.

CHAPTER 52 *Seventh Generation*

Children of James Louis Hamrick and wife, Sarah McSwain Brunitia married John Moore. Cora married Asa Lovelace, second husband Perry Humphries.

CHAPTER 53. *Sixth Generation*

Children of Elijah Hamrick and wife, Hannah Hamrick· Noah married Mary Narcissus Hamrick Wiley married Matilda Green. Elijah married Pathenia Green. Margaret married se J. Mc-

ANOTHER TYPE OF EARLY COTTON GIN.   (SEE PAGE 27)

Murly. Sarah married Joseph Green. Nancy never married. Jane never married. Andrew Jackson never married. David never married. Perry never married

CHAPTER 54. *Seventh Generation.*

Children of Noah Hamrick and wife, Mary Narcissus Hamrick: Carvus married Amanda Lovelace. Wellington married Beufer McCraw. Galena married Thomas Jolley. Essie married Everett Goode Pinkney married Rosanna Lee. Jasper not married.

CHAPTER 55 *Seventh Generation.*

Children of Wiley Hamrick and wife, Matilda Green: Duke married Ida Holland.

CHAPTER 56 *Seventh Generation*

Children of Elijah Hamrick and wife, Patheney Green. Bruno not married.

CHAPTER 57. *Seventh Generation*

Children of Joseph Green and wife, Sarah Hamrick: Solon married Catherine Hamrick Andrew Jackson married Permelia Green. Patience married George Green McSwain. Charles Jefferson never married.

CHAPTER 58 *Seventh Generation.*

Children of Jesse J McMurry and wife, Margaret Hamrick: Andrew Simeon married Irene Suttle. Avery Winslow married Cora Willis. Hannah married Honey Illiff Washburn

CHAPTER 59 *Sixth Generation*

Children of George Robertson Hamrick and wife, Rebecca Hamrick. Sarah Ann Margaret never married. Nancy Jane never married.

Children of George Robertson Hamrick and wife, Elvira Hamrick: Drury Pleasant married Susanna Hamrick Burton married Florence

Dickson   William Clinton married Elizabeth Lee   Clearendy married Green Gold Lovelace.   Mary Alice married Amose Wright McSwain.   Rockaney married Wesley Lee   Pinkney never married.

Chapter 60   *Sixth Generation.*

Children of Jonathan McSwain Hamrick and wife, Elizabeth Hamrick.   George Pinkney married Sarah Anthony.   Charles Elam married Eugenia Pruett.   Margaret married Junius Costner Lovelace.   Hannah married David Scruggs.   Rosanna married Moses Wood   James Crowder never married   Melton Webb never married.   Asbury never married   Eunice never married   John Sylvanus never married.   Sara Lucindy never married.   Loueasy married James Pruett (no children)

Chapter 61.   *Seventh Generation*

Children of George Pinkney Hamrick and wife, Sarah Anthony.
Earl married Adele Geier

Chapter 62.   *Seventh Generation*

Children of Charles Elam Hamrick and wife, Eugenia Pruett:
Jonothan married Mississippi Jones; second wife, Bertha Davis.
Clyde married Daisy Green.   Eunie married Lenora Hopper   Dollie married Robert Stover   Clarence married Ida Jones

Chapter 63.   *Sixth Generation.*

Children of John Judson Jones and wife, Nancy Hamrick: Cynthia Catherine never married   Elijah Edmon married Eunice Hardin   William Asbury married Sarah Moore.   Reuben married Maremley Kirby, second wife, Laura Lee   Drury Pinkney married Sarah McDaniel.   Josie Gilbert married Sarah Harrell, second wife, Sarah Elizabeth Davis   Liddie Jane married Eli Davis, second husband Oliver Haynes   John Kendrick married Roseline McDaniel, second wife, Bernice Lowery.   Stephen Collins married Eunice Wilson Jones.   Leander Judson married Margaret Allen; second wi . . . . Short. fourth wife,

Sarah Grady.   Joseph Newton married Elizabeth Quinn.   John Ezell never married.   Alvie Alexander never married.

CHAPTER 64. *Seventh Generation*

Children of Elijah Edmon Jones and wife Eunice Hardin· John Jesse married Victoria Webb   Columbus Alexander married Mindia Bridges   Laura Etta never married   Fannie Roxanna married Thomas Murk.   Hannah Margaret married John Skinner.   William Wesley married Flora Bailey.   Nancy Loueasy married Willie Owens. Mary Catherine married Colon Wright   George Lee married Mary Philbeck   Zillie Jane married Cicero Melton   Tenna Elizabeth married John Wilson.   Joseph not married.

CHAPTER 65   *Seventh Generation.*

Children of William Asbury Jones and wife, Sarah Moore   John Blanton married Nancy Brown; second wife, Darcus Stegall   James Clarence married Ida Hamrick.   Sarah Elender married George Lookadoo Pruett   Eulter Mathue married Alice Blanton.   William Sylvannus married Frances Fulton.   Horace Columbus married Mamie Bridges   Georgia Mozell married John Davis   Farmer Moore never married.   Maneivey Catherine never married   Colton Eldridge married Bessie Warren.   Nancy not married

CHAPTER 66. *Seventh Generation.*

Children of Reuben Wilson Jones and wife, Maremley Kirby. Nancy Caroline married Hugh C Wray   Susanna Catherine married Allen Robert Kelley   Thomas Henry married Pearl Smith John never married.

CHAPTER 67. *Seventh Generation.*

Children of Drury Pinkney Jones and wife, Sarah McDaniel· Charles Alexander married Bell Hollifield, second wife, Emma E Knowles.   Sidney Crowder married Sarah Sparks.   Berry Austin married Nolie Wilson   Eliza never married.   Lula Eetta married William Hollifield   John Crayton not married

CHAPTER 68. *Seventh Generation.*

Children of Josie Gilbert Jones and wife, Sarah Hartell. George Batie married Bell Wray. Nathaniel Louis married Clara Berry; second wife, Lela McMellon. Mississippi married Jonothan Hamrick. Essic Estella married Flay Green. Ella L married James Workman. Addie not married. Ada Lee never married. Seven infants.

CHAPTER 69. *Seventh Generation.*

Children of Eli Davis and wife, Liddie Jane Jones: Monroe married Queen Victoria Gibbs. Cicero married Pansy Allen. Hester married Lawson Melton.

CHAPTER 70. *Seventh Generation*

Children of John Kendrick Jones and wife, Roseline McDaniels. Leroy Hampton married Missouri Rodgers. Landrum Decatur married Loney Moore

Children of John Kendrick Jones and wife, Bernice Lowery: Ora not married. Straucey Catherine not married

CHAPTER 71 *Seventh Generation.*

Children of Stephen Collis Jones and wife, Eunice Wilson Jones: Hilda Jane married Doctor Seaton Jones. Elisha Edgar married Effie Hamrick, second wife, Lillie Wall. Silas Gold married Lillie Smith. John Alvie married Lillie Benton. Nancy Priscilla married Durant Pressley. Lawrence Welborn married Ola Rumfelt. Joseph Benjamin Hall married Polly Pressley

CHAPTER 72 *Seventh Generation.*

Children of Leander Judson Jones and wife, Lucindy Brown: Minnie Lee married John Terry. Georgeanna married Archie Newman. John Judson married Fannie Neblett. Four infants.

Children of Leander Judson Jones and wife, Ida Short: Claud married Matilda Sauter. Lula May not married. Joseph not married

CHAPTER 73. *Seventh Generation*

Children of Joseph Newton Jones and wife, Elizabeth Quinn Thomas Judson married Lillie Goode. Clara married Landrum Collins. Bernard B. married Carroll Jane Nanney. Susanna Bell married Chivus Earley. Delois married Fredrick Jones.

CHAPTER 74. *Sixth Generation.*

Children of Reuben Hamrick and wife, Phoebia Hamrick: Charles Clingman married Maggie Wilson. Susanna married George Champion McSwain. Sarah married Leander Sheppard Hamrick.

CHAPTER 75. *Seventh Generation.*

Children of Charles Clingman Hamrick and wife, Maggie Wilson: Fuller married Pauline Olive. Gertrude married Peter Grigg Oren not married.

CHAPTER 76. *Sixth Generation*

Children of Drury Harrell and wife, Jane Hamrick Louisa Elizabeth married Sidney Hill Hamrick Eliza married Willard Winslow Washburn Roseline married Chauncey Abram Washburn.

CHAPTER 77. *Fifth Generation.*

Children of John Hamrick and wife, Barbara Maruney Edmond married Nancy Bostic. Robert married Hannah Dobbins Jane married Thomas Pruett Jesse never married. Martin never married. Rebecca never married.

CHAPTER 78 *Sixth Generation.*

Children of Edmon Hamrick and wife, Nancy Bostic· Drury married Ammie McKinney William married Jane Hamrick. Chesley married Matilda O'Neal, second wife. Nancy Walker, third wife, Sarah Ann Green Elizabeth married John McKinney. Sarah married John McSwain. Narcissus married Martin Weathers. Eunice married Berry Green

Chapter 79 *Seventh Generation*

Children of Drury Hamrick and wife, Annie McKinney. Mary Ann married Richard Cogdell, second husband, Perry Cogdell. Julia Ann married William Jasper Jones (no children). Biddie Ann married Thomas Buchannan   Martha Ann never married

Chapter 80. *Seventh Generation.*

Children of Chesley Hamrick and wife, Nancy Walker   Edmond married Carolina Hamrick. Martha married Lawson Brooks   Bryson married Eliza Barnett   Lucindy married James Green. Elizabeth married John Nolan   Drury married Susanna Stroup   John never married

Children of Chesley Hamrick and wife, Sarah Ann Green. Rosanna married John Morrow. Doxie married John Quinn Padgett

Chapter 81 *Sixth Generation*

Children of Robert Hamrick and wife, Hannah Dobbins   James Louis married Elizabeth Hamrick   Robert Benson married Emiline Horne. Cook married Louisa Jane Dobbins   Thomas married Mary Earl (no children). Emiline Rencie married Isam Horne   Rachael never married

Chapter 82 *Seventh Generation*

Children of Cook Hamrick and wife Louisa Jane Dobbins· Barney McMahan married Caroline Henry   James Marcellus married Mamie Eli   McLanton married Josie Wright   Octavia married James Louis Hamrick. Luvenia married Braxton Wall   Dora married George Dobson   Frances Marion married Mollie Freeman   Lenna married ———— Haney. Prerarie never married.

Chapter 83 *Seventh Generation*

Children of Isam Horne and wife, Emiline Rencie Hamrick   Thomas married Eliza Price   Susanna married James Campe   Carrie m . . .   . Horton

Braxton married Sarah Bostic   Joseph married Susanna. Crow. John never married

Chapter 84 *Seventh Generation.*

Children of James Louis Hamrick and wife, Elizabeth Hamrick: Albert married Phoebia Wammock   James Louis married Octavia Hamrick   Cicero married Sarah Smiley

Chapter 85. *Seventh Generation.*

Children of Robert Hamrick and wife, Emiline Horne. Landrum married Martha Davis. Martha married John Davis. Hannah married Curtis Wall. Julia married Andrew McGinnis. Alfie married Monroe Hollifield. Malindy never married

Chapter 86. *Sixth Generation.*

Children of William Hamrick and wife, Jane Hamrick: Asa married Caroline Bridges (no children) Nancy Susanna married Wiley Bridges, second husband, Chesley Bostic.

Chapter 87. *Seventh Generation.*

Children of Wiley Bridges and wife. Nancy Susanna Hamrick: Joseph Suttles married Alice Hamrick

Chapter 88. *Seventh Generation.*

Children of John McKinney and wife, Elizabeth Hamrick: Narcissus married Louis Scoggins. Martha married Alonzo Rollins Josiah Durhan never married.

Chapter 89 *Seventh Generation.*

Children of Martin Weather and wife, Narcissus Hamrick: Glover married Eunice Quinn, second wife, Sara Ann Green. Nancy married Alfred Hamrick   Priscilla married William Boswell McSwain Laura married Hamilton Jenkins; second husband, Albert Cicero Bridges. John married Annie Wall. Willie Monroe married Sarah

Blanton; second wife, Millie Green   Rebecca married Columbus McCraw   Charles married Cynthis Barnett

CHAPTER 90 Seventh Generation.

Children of Berry Green and wife, Eunice Hamrick. John married Hesentine Cudd. Roxanna married Bryson Green   George Thomas married Judia Cleary   Dora Jane married Hackett Wall Harvey Hatcher married Jane Lee   James Andrew never married

CHAPTER 91 Sixth Generation.

Children of Thomas Pruett and wife, Jane Hamrick· William married Adeline Webb   John married Susanna Holland. Perry married Susanna Earl   Wiley S. married Hannah Earl. Thomas married Mary Hughes (no children). James Crowder married Mary Jolley. Almedia married Alfred Turner (no children)   Jane never married   Lucindy never married

CHAPTER 92. Seventh Generation.

Children of William Pruett and wife, Adeline Webb: John married Sarah Beam.

CHAPTER 93. Seventh Generation.

Children of John Pruett and wife, Susanna Holland. Perry Henderson married Hannah Lovelace   Lemuel M married Maggie Shaw   James L married Louise Hamrick, second wife, Ella Kirby Thomas married Maggie Sperlin. Greenberry B married Maggie Sperlin   Permelia married James Louis Lovelace. Eugenia married Charles Elam Hamrick. Gold Griffin never married   Sarah never married. Doctor Melvin never married

CHAPTER 94. Seventh Generation

Children of Wiley Pruett and wife, Hannah Earl   John Jethro married Elizabeth Green. Elizabeth Jane married Ruphus Pinkney Weathers. George Lookadoo married Susanna Blanton, second wife, Sara Elle   ιι   · ιιι,ι ι   ιι   Madison

D married Eliza Griffin Roxanna married George Washington Lovelace. Alice Docia married Thomas Plonk.

CHAPTER 95. *Seventh Generation*

Children of Crowder Pruett and wife, Mary Jolley. James Crowder married Patience Tate Almedia married Oliver Newton Hamrick (no children) Dora married James Lee McSwain Roseline married Landrum Jolley. Thomas never married. Jesse never married. Essie never married.

CHAPTER 96 *Seventh Generation*

Children of Perry Pruett and wife, Susanna Earl· Thomas Newton married Francis Beheeler, second wife, Ada Horne, third wife, Fannie Hamrick Rachael Jane married Gilead Green. William Cicero married Maggie Fergusson. Francis Marion married Mary Latham.

CHAPTER 97. *Fifth Generation*

Children of Reuben Hamrick and wife, Hannah McSwain George married Mary Hamrick William married Martha McSwain. Asa married Drucindy Bridges; second wife. Mary Hughes Berry married Catherine Hamrick, second wife. Celia Pannell, third wife, Delphia Hardin Narcissus married James Green. Rebecca married Elias Green. Judith married James Lovelace. Mary married Louis McSwain. Elizabeth married Jonothan McSwain Hamrick. Sarah never married

CHAPTER 98 *Sixth Generation.*

Children of George Hamrick and wife. Mary Hamrick. Amos married Judy Allen Doctor Noah married Eliza Matheney; second wife, Evelyne Blanton Elias married Lucindy Wilkie. Greenberry married Mary Owen Jahue married Elizabeth Green Eli married Sarah Anne Green. Hannah married Isaac Hollifield Sarah Minervia married John Green Jayson married Sarah Anne Blanton Wiley married Sarah Matheney John Landrum never married Archibald never married Louis never married.

CHAPTER 99. *Seventh Generation*

Children of Amos Hamrick and wife, Judia Allen· Norman married Elizabeth Dedmon. Mary married Alcie Green Randall. John never married.

CHAPTER 100. *Seventh Generation*

Children of Doctor Noah Hamrick and wife, Eliza Matheney: Elizabeth never married

Children of Doctor Noah Hamrick and wife, Evelyne Blanton. Sarah married Pinkney Bridges George married Josephine Blanton. Elijah married Effie Goforth Arrie married Shaw Randall. Charles married Minnie Walker. Claudie married Shaw Randall Ida married Thomas Goforth. Clyde married Maudie Hambright. Blanch married Beaufort Randall Howard not married Corene not married

CHAPTER 101. *Seventh Generation*

Children of Elias Hamrick and wife, Lucindy Wilkie. Panthia married Shaw Randall Eliza married Mascoe Wease Ola married Noah Green. George married Maggie Beam Emiline married Charles Dobbins. Mattie married Joseph Blanton

CHAPTER 102. *Seventh Generation*

Children of Greenberry Hamrick and wife, Mary Owens. Wiley married Martha Baily Luther married Permelia McKinney; second wife, Johnnie Hamrick; third wife. Susanna Webb

CHAPTER 103. *Seventh Generation.*

Children of Jehu Hamrick and wife, Elizabeth Green· James Louis married Josie Bridges. Greenberry married Nancy Green Mary married Milas Hawkins Nancy Jane married Edgar Hollifield Asa married Eva Padgett Clayton married Ella Lanchaster. Gilford married Maudie Cole Edith married Seth Hamrick Lemuel Eli nev·   ·   ··   ·   ··

CHAPTER 104. *Seventh Generation*

Children of Eli Hamrick and wife, Sarah Ann Green: Jane married George Hill. Seth married Edith Bostic; second wife, Edith Hamrick. David married Lula Robbins. Margaret married Leander Burns; second husband, George Hill. Hannah Sarah never married. One infant.

CHAPTER 105 *Seventh Generation*

Children of Isaac Hollifield and wife, Hannah Hamrick. Edgar married Allie Allen; second wife, Nancy Jane Hamrick.

CHAPTER 106 *Seventh Generation*

Children of John Green and wife, Sarah Mincivia Hamrick: Noah married Ora Hamrick. Roxanna married George Blanton; second husband, Andrew Higgins. Marenda married William James. Hannah married Joseph Brooks. Monroe married Savannah Turner. Luther married Laura Harvey. Asa married Susanna Higgins.

CHAPTER 107. *Seventh Generation.*

Children of Jason Hamrick and wife Sarah Ann Blanton: Nancy married Frankin Blanton

CHAPTER 108 *Seventh Generation.*

Children of Wiley Hamrick and wife, Sarah Ann Matheney: Roxanna married George Hill.

CHAPTER 109. *Sixth Generation*

Children of William Hamrick and wife, Martha McSwain. Cassie married David Oliver Green.

CHAPTER 110 *Sixth Generation.*

Children of James Green and wife, Narcissus Hamrick: Elias married Rebecca Rollins. Rueben married Judith Green. George married Martha Rollins; second wife, Elizabeth McKinney; third wife, Eliza Black. Ewell married Catherine Green. Noah married

7

Nancy Cawhorne   Asa married Millie Green   Berry married Jane Owens   James Moore married Hannah McSwain   Elizabeth married Jahen Hamrick.   William married Rebecca Champion; second wife, Nancy Green.   Judith married Benjamin Franklin McSwain. Nancy married Martin Earl   Edmond never married   Hannah never married.   One infant

CHAPTER 111. *Seventh Generation.*

Children of Elias Green and wife, Rebecca Rollins   Bryson married Roxanna Green; second wife, Susanna Allison.   Malissa married Richard Jolley.   Jane married Edley Jolley   Cordelia married William Hicks, second husband, Louis Hamrick   Malindy married David Hamrick Moore   Webb married Ella Elliott.   Hill married Ella Wilson.   Doctor married Susanna Bridges.   Monroe married Mittie Cleary   James married Ada Reace.

CHAPTER 112   *Seventh Generation.*

Children of Reuben Green and wife, Judith Green.   Noah married Fannie Pearson; second wife, Margaret Hamrick; third wife, Patience Bridges.   Joseph married Ricey Gatheria Hamrick   John married Lucindy Green, second wife, Mary Green, third wife, Nancy Byers   Judith married Willis Green   Pathenia married Elijah Hamrick   Hesentine married Berry Ezell McSwain.   Hannah never married

CHAPTER 113   *Seventh Generation*

Children of George Green and wife, Martha Rollins·   Jefferson Wright married Susanna Jolley.   Noah married Jane Bridges (no children)   Rebecca married Zechariah Dobbins Harrell.   Marion never married.   Ellen never married.   Adeline never married.   Narcissus never married.

CHAPTER 114   *Seventh Generation*

Children of Green Green and wife, Jane Owens·   Zorah married

James Collins   Martha married Elisha Hinson   James Willis married Cora Scruggs.   Mary Ellen never married.

Chapter 115. *Seventh Generation*

Children of Asa Green and wife, Millie Green: Ida married Thomas Goode.

Chapter 116 *Seventh Generation*

Children of James Moore Green and wife, Hannah McSwain: Gilead married Rachael Jane Pruett, second wife, Susannah Hamrick   Reuben married Catherine Murrell   Preston married Sarah Hopper.   Senith married William Neal; second husband, Ruphus Gladden.

Chapter 117. *Seventh Generation.*

Children of William Green and wife, Rebecca Champion: James married Lucindy Hamrick   Dixon married Rebecca Green   Roda married Thomas Blanton. Nancy married Benjamin Justice. George never married.

Children of William Green and wife, Nancy Green.   Willis married Mary Ann Green.   Jane married Asa Green. Rebecca married Jacob Tate, second husband, Williamson Brindell   Cleo married William Glasgow   Hannah married Joseph Robertson

Chapter 118. *Seventh Generation.*

Children of Martin Earls and wife, Nancy Green.   Willis married Cora Scruggs. Narcissus married Elijah Ledbetter. William married Mary Ramsey. Elizabeth married James Colver Green. Rosilla married Robert Padgett.

Chapter 119. *Sixth Generation*

Children of Elias Green and wife, Rebecca Hamrick. Benjamin married Susanna Elmore   Reuben married Jane Scruggs. Berry married Eunice Hamrick. Albert married Mary Jane Washburn, second wife, Zuba Durham. Thomas married Susanna McSwain

Judith married Volney Goode   Hannah married James Wood   Drucindy married John Green   Jonothan married Louisa Wood. Sarah married David Scruggs. Mary never married. Harvey never married.

CHAPTER 120   *Seventh Generation*

Children of Albert Green and wife, Mary Jane Washburn· Cora never married.

CHAPTER 121. *Seventh Generation.*

Children of Reuben Green and wife, Jane Scruggs· Toliver married Johnnie Burge   Robert Lee married Elizabeth Jolley   Jonothan married Blanch Hamrick   Seaton married Susanna Canton   Murphy married Erie Pearson   Permelia married Andrew Green   Kansas married Chivus Bridges. Volney never married   Albert never married   Two infants.

CHAPTER 122. *Seventh Generation*

Children of Volney Goode and wife, Judith Green· Oscar married Nolla Pope. Ollie married Franklin Weathers   Elsie married Rex McCraw. Charles married Susanna Wilson, second wife, Patience Tate   Eunice married Cluff McSwain   Tony married Ernest Burton Lovelace. George married Julia Painter. Thomas married Ida Green.

CHAPTER 123. *Seventh Generation.*

Children of James Wood and wife, Hannah Green   Moses married Rosanna Hamrick, second wife, Rosanna Ledbetter   Eunice married Gabriel Ellis. Mary Susanna married William Skinner. Rebecca married Aaron Reuben Hamrick. Three infants.

CHAPTER 124. *Seventh Generation.*

Children of Jonothan Green and wife, Louisa Wood. Ida married John Pruett. Docia married Plato Brooks   Rebecca married Lawrence Rollins. Willard married Dovia Scoggins. Melvin married Lillie B---d. ---- never married

Chapter 125. *Seventh Generation.*

Children of Benjamin Green and wife, Susanna Elmore: Octavia married George Hawkins. Penina married George Matheney. Mary Jane married Drury Dobbins Hamrick.

Chapter 126. *Sixth Generation.*

Children of Asa Hamrick and wife, Drucindy Bridges: Aaron Reuben married Massie Byers; second wife Rebecca Wood. Jabez married Martha Durham, second wife, Kisiah McDaniel; third wife, Mahalie Surratt. Drury Joseph married Elizabeth Nicholson. Dr. Timmons Greenberry married Cora Lovelace, second wife, Mary Harrell. Rosanna married Capt. Oliver Holland. Hannah Sarah married David Matheney. Cordelia married Asa Monroe Lovelace. Susanna never married. Cynthia never married.

Chapter 127 *Seventh Generation.*

Children of Jabez Hamrick and wife, Martha Durham: Thedocia married Manda White. Susanna married Drury Pleasant Hamrick. Edwin B. married Ocie Foy Hamrick.

Chapter 128. *Seventh Generation.*

Children of Aaron Reuben Hamrick and wife, Massie Byers: Brodus married Antonnettie Bridges. Missouri married James Mc-Swain. Susanna Veltazer married Asbury Webb. Georgie not married.

Chapter 129 *Seventh Generation*

Children of Drury Joseph Hamrick and wife, Elizabeth Nicholson: Clarence married Myrtle Hamrick. Blanch married Jonas Green. Nancy married John Cash. Bertha married Julius Davis. Maudie married Nebbet Kendrick. Dr. John A. married Catherine Kushtattler. Mary never married. Grace never married.

Chapter 130. *Seventh Generation*

Children of Capt. Oliver Holland and wife, Rosanna Hamrick

Dr. Bezolan married Lillie Hull   Permelia married John Hopper. Williamson never married

Chapter 131   *Seventh Generation.*

Children of Dr. Timmons Greenberry Hamrick and wife, Cora Lovelace: Forest Gains married Carrie Thompson. Malgrim Flay married Maude Michael. Cora Anne not married

Children of Dr. Timmons Greenberry Hamrick and wife, Mary Harrell· Timmons Rhoe not married. Asa Harrell not married.

Chapter 132   *Fifth Generation.*

Children of Samuel Hamrick and wife, Susanna Adams   William married Narcissus Hughes   Adroniram married Nancy Dobbins Burwell married Nancy Elizabeth Hughes. Asa married Edith Scoggins, second wife Nancy Christmas. Nancy married Starlin Hughes   Elizabeth married James Louis Hamrick   Susanna married Simon Davis. Madeline married Allen Cogdell. Jane married William Hamrick   Mary never married.

Chapter 133   *Sixth Generation*

Children of William Hamrick and wife, Narcissus Hughes   Samuel Young married Sarah Turner. Martha Elvira married George Robertson Hamrick. Mary Narcissus married Noah Hamrick. Sarah married Williamson Lee. Nancy Dianna married Landrum L. Smith. Susanna married Andy Hamrick; second husband George Bowens Putnam Myers never married. Vestie Victoria married General Moore   Julia Malindy never married. Margaret Jane never married   Lucindy never married. William never married

Chapter 134.   *Seventh Generation*

Children of Samuel Young Hamrick and wife, Sarah Turner: Rush married Etta Putnam. Dora Etta married Thomas Goode. Boswell Hill married Rilla Moore   Thomas Grover married Lottie Ledbetter   Martha Jane married Henry Smith   Louisa Coy married Ora Green   Claude Franklin married Mont Crawford. Augusta Emeline married Baylus Proctor   Docia Ellen married Jesse Hawkins   Nelson never married   Kansas never married.   Two infants.

CHAPTER 135. *Sixth Generation.*

Children of Adroniram Hamrick and wife, Nancy Dobbins: William married Margaret McDaniel; second wife, Cora Simmons. Martha married Thomas Canady (no children).   Almedia married William McDaniel.   Kisiah married Thomas Thombs, second husband, James Green.   Vinson Dobbins married Mary Jane Green. Louis married Lettie Wammac.   Albert married Julia Webb.

CHAPTER 136. *Seventh Generation.*

Children of William McDonniel and wife, Almedia Hamrick: Monroe married Ada Moore   Burrus married Lucindy Williamson. Madison married Edith Helton.   Dollie married Robert Carroll. Julius married Ida Moore.   Cantus married Florence Griffin.   Sarah married Alonzo Bostic.   Essie married Garland Shull   Zulia married John Carroll.   Joseph Crayton never married.   One infant.

CHAPTER 137. *Seventh Generation.*

Children of Vinson Dobbins Hamrick and wife, Mary Jane Green: Gallena married Millard Fisher.   Cletus married Callie Free   Susanna married Coran Hardin   Oscar married Dovie Canady   Alonzo married Carrie McSwain   Elsie married Herbert Smith   Carron married Ada Wells.   Vallie married Webb Lookado   Howard never married.   Walter not married.   Mamie not married

CHAPTER 138. *Seventh Generation.*

Children of Albert Hamrick and wife, Julia Webb·   George Pinkney married Nancy Smith.   Nancy married James Brown. Lishie not married   Russell not married.   Mary never married.

CHAPTER 139 *Sixth Generation*

Children of Burwell Hamrick and wife, Nancy Elizabeth Hughes:

Hill married Eunice Jane McSwain. Landrum never married James never married Mary Jane never married.

Chapter 140. *Seventh Generation.*

Children of Hill Hamrick and wife, Eunice Jane McSwain: John Landrum married Docia Green. Gidney married Ida Harrell. Andrew Miller married Elizabeth Green Thomas Burwell married Margaret Blanton; second wife, Hester Green David married Bell Wood. Solon married Cora Beam. George married Cleopatra McSwain Elsie married William Bridges Leander married Lena Spratt Broadus not married Hannah not married.

Chapter 141. *Sixth Generation*

Children of Asa Hamrick and wife, Edith Scoggins· Terpin Goode married Sarah Jane Baber. Louise married Louis Doggett. Lafayette married Elizabeth Moore. John married Emma McDonnel

Chapter 142. *Seventh Generation.*

Children of Lafayette Hamrick and wife, Elizabeth Moore: Asa Vance married Emma Hinson. Doctor Louis married Dollie Wommack. John Lafayette married Viola Hardin Morris never married. Two infants

Chapter 143. *Seventh Generation*

Children of Terpin Goode Hamrick and wife, Mary Jane Baber Broadus married Carrie Bergin Attie married Harris Coffee Cora married Bost Dean Dora married Doctor Crawley. Ezell married Ida Hardin Mamie married John Johnston Earl married Laura Bell Cash. Agnes married James Baber Myrtle never married

Chapter 144 *Seventh Generation.*

Children of John Hamrick and wife, Emma McDaniel Mamie married Columbus Pritchard Penina married Levi Ellis. Elsie married J d Nelson Pritchard. Rebecca married James Dearman.

EARLY TYPE OF COTTON GIN. (SEE PAGE 27)

Edith married William Dunn. Asa Alburtie married Mary Carroll. Mary married Franklin Swann. Bertie married —— Burleson. Ocie not married

CHAPTER 145. *Seventh Generation*

Children of Ruphus Doggett and wife, Louise Hamrick. Edith married Robert Griffin. Nancy married Rolley Hardin. Leroy married Mattie Sorrells Ida married Quince Jones George married Gatheria Huntley. Cora married Luther Morrow. Durham never married.

CHAPTER 146. *Sixth Generation*

Children of Starlin Hughes and wife, Nancy Hamrick· William married Martha Turner Jane married Nelson Watterson. Susanna married Fennell Patterson Malindy married Rush Gladden Elizabeth married William Coggins. McKenzie never married Julia never married. Jefferson never married.

CHAPTER 147. *Seventh Generation.*

Children of Nelson Watterson and wife, Jane Hughes: John married Elizabeth Howell. Hope married Martha Ware. Magby married Rebecca Howell Mary married Martin Hicks

CHAPTER 148 *Seventh Generation*

Children of Ruphus Gladden and wife, Malindy Hughes: James married Julia Johnston Clarence married Alma Kerr.

CHAPTER 149. *Seventh Generation.*

Children of Fennell Patterson and wife, Susanna Hughes Thomas married Susanna Camp; second wife, Charity Biggerstaff. William married Della Edwards John married Fannie Wilson. Lemuel married Docia Smith. Julius married Margaret Morrison. Junie married Thomas Camp. Mary married John Glover Docia married Grover H. ll

CHAPTER 150. *Seventh Generation.*

Children of Albert Hamrick and wife, Phoebia Wommack: Bynum married Elsie Walker   Roy married Maggie Shyttle   Hoyel married Beula Hoyle.   Susanna married Elbert Dobbins   Phoebia married Decatur Early.   Mary married Oscar Wright   Josie married Evans Dobbins.   Three infants.

CHAPTER 151   *Sixth Generation.*

Children of Simon Davis and wife, Susanna Hamrick   Franklin married Lucindy Sheppard   Noah married Ella Robertson.   Bryson married Ida Inman   Monroe married Doua Davis.   Malindy married John Moore   Julia never married.

CHAPTER 152.   *Sixth Generation*

Children of Allen Cogdell and wife, Madaline Hamrick.   Martha married Crayton Lovelace   Nancy never married   Ensley never married   Five infants.

CHAPTER 153   *Fifth Generation*

Children of David Hamrick and wife, Rebecca Raney: Archibal married Sarah Webb.

Children of David Hamrick and wife, Sarah McSwain   Moore married Mary Green   Mary married George Hamrick   Elizabeth married John Matheney   Sarah married David Hamrick   Eliza married Benjamin Green.   Hannah married Elijah Hamrick   Rebecca married George Robertson Hamrick.   Elijah married Millie McSwain   Judith never married   Nancy never married

CHAPTER 154.   *Sixth Generation*

Children of Archibal Hamrick and wife, Sarah Webb.   James married Rosanna Lovelace   David married Lucindy Powell.   Elijah married Emiline Webb   Alfred married Nancy Weathers   Nancy married Peal Canady.   Martha married Perry Blanton   Sarah married Wiley Lovelace.   second husband, Matthew Sperlin.   Mary married George Matheney; second husband, John Canady. Malissa married James Nolan. Rebecca married James Champion Roseanna married Kenneth Blanton. Angaline never married. Elizabeth never married.

CHAPTER 155. *Seventh Generation*

Children of James Hamrick and wife, Rosanna Lovelace: Nathaniel Archibald married Hester Melton Monroe married Effie Webb. Biddie married Nolvey Lovelace.

CHAPTER 156 *Seventh Generation*

Children of Alfred Hamrick and wife, Nancy Weathers· Broadus married Bessie Bailey. George married Gertrude Putnam. Ethel married George Dover.

CHAPTER 157. *Seventh Generation.*

Children of Elijah Hamrick and wife, Emiline Webb Christopher married Cordelia McSwain. Narcissus married George McSwain.

CHAPTER 158 *Seventh Generation.*

Children of David Hamrick and wife, Lucindy Powell John B. married Laura Byers Louis married Harris Rippy, second wife, Maggie Dixon. Sarah married McCager Mauney Carolina married Edmond Hamrick. Susanna married John Rippy.

CHAPTER 159. *Seventh Generation*

Children of Peal Canady and wife, Nancy Hamrick Fredrick married Rosanna Digh. Rody married Perry Couch. Four infants.

CHAPTER 160. *Seventh Generation.*

Children of Kenneth Blanton and wife, Rosanna Hamrick: Dora married Joseph Powell. Sarah married Scott McMahan Hessie married Scott McMahan Doxie married Robert Biggerstaff. Hoyle never married

CHAPTER 161. *Seventh Generation.*

Children of James Nolan and wife, Malissa Hamrick: Sarah married William Joseph Green. Mary married Willis Green. John married Elizabeth Hamrick. David married Ola Champion.

CHAPTER 162. *Seventh Generation*

Children of James Champion and wife, Rebecca Hamrick. William married Lucindy Johnston. Mary married William Short. Beattie married Hattie McCoy; second wife, May Davis George married Loney Ross. Tisha married Alfred Lindsay Frankie married Phillip Scism.

CHAPTER 163. *Seventh Generation.*

Children of Perry Blanton and wife, Martha Hamrick: Joseph married Mattie Hamrick Thomas married Ida O'Brien. George married Lillie Butler. John married Willie Harrell Elijah married Lula Randall. Jane married John Harrell Margaret married Thomas Hamrick. Elizabeth never married. Ransom never married.

CHAPTER 164. *Sixth Generation.*

Children of Moore Hamrick and wife, Mary Green· David married Sarah Moore. Sarah married Rollie Roberts. Nancy married David Green. Henry married Amanda Holland. Judith married Elijah Green. Susanna married Chamber Wood Aaron married Susanna Wood Eliza never married

CHAPTER 165 *Seventh Generation.*

Children of Rollie Roberts and wife, Sarah Hamrick: William married Louisa Gillespie Ezra married Jane Green Mary Anne married Richard Hughes Nancy married Julius Goode

CHAPTER 166. *Seventh Generation*

Children of David Hamrick and wife, Sarah Moore· Thomas married Susanna Jolley. James Marida married Pathenia Hopper.

Louis married Cordelia Green   Franklin married Susanna Hamrick, second wife, Elsie Humphries; third wife, Susanna Humphries John married Ida Hamrick. Leah Jane married Alvy Jones. Sarah married Hilary Jolley   Leander married Della Surratt. Eunice married William Hawkins. Mary married Moses Scruggs

CHAPTER 167 *Seventh Generation*

Children of Henry Hamrick and wife, Amanda Holland. Gilford married Tolitha Holland   James married Jane Jolley. Mary Jane married Jackson Jolley. Martha married Robert Jones Charles married Assill McCombs. David never married.

CHAPTER 168 *Seventh Generation.*

Children of Aaron Hamrick and wife, Susanna Goode. James William married Turie Haynes, second wife, ——— Scruggs.

CHAPTER 169 *Seventh Generation*

Children of Chambers Wood and wife, Susanna Hamrick: Walter married Susanna Green.

CHAPTER 170. *Fourth Generation.*

Children of James Bridges and wife, Rebecca Hamrick· Samuel married Rebecca Hamrick, second wife, Mollie Hamrick. Aaron married Sarah Hamrick   John married Elizabeth Bridges   Nancy married Price Hamrick. Margaret married George Blanton (no children). Frankie married Thomas McSwain. Mary married William McSwain   Phoebia Margaret married Burwell Blanton. Vianna married Henry Ledbetter. Nancy married Benjamin Hughes. Burwell married Nancy Elizabeth Harmon. James married Elizabeth Hamrick   George married Mary Matheney. Elizabeth married William Bridges   Asa never married. Richard never married.

CHAPTER 171 *Fifth Generation*

Children of Samuel Bridges and wife, Rebecca Hamrick   Jesse married E-- -- Hart-- -- -- -- M-- -- Dye.

Children of Samuel Bridges and wife, Mollie Hamrick: John married Cinthia Jones. Caleb married Nancy Young Washington married Artie Hamrick. Mary married Robbin Green. Sarah married Louis Sparks Susanna married Calvin Sparks Reuben married Cinthia McSwain. Charlotte married Edward Parish Jones Rebecca never married. Elizabeth never married.

CHAPTER 172. *Sixth Generation*

Children of Jesse Bridges and wife, Elizabeth Harrell: Samuel married Marian Pinson, second wife, Nancy Green. Frankie married Marion Hamrick. Elmira married Street Hamrick

Children of Jesse Bridges and wife Malindy Dye: Jsse Whitston married Jane Hamrick Reuben married Margaret Mauney Gold; second wife, Alice Washburn. Sarah Jane married William F. Barnett.

CHAPTER 173 *Seventh Generation*

Children of Jesse Whitston Bridges and wife, Jane Hamrick: Samuel married Aquilla Hamrick. Cicero married Leona Magness. Charles married Missouri Bridges Lora married Jesse Blanton, second husband, Albert Johnston Clarence married Cleo Washburn. Summey never married.

CHAPTER 174. *Seventh Generation*

Children of Reuben Bridges and wife, Margaret Mauney Gold· Robert married Nancy Sigmon, second wife, Laura Lee. Nola married Oliver Beaty Hamrick. Laura married John Epley Champion. John married James Stevens Florence Gaither never married Cora never married.

CHAPTER 175 *Seventh Generation.*

Children of William F Barnett and wife, Sarah Jane Bridges. Jesse married Eva Wilson. James married Amanda Chitwood. Panthia married Richard Champion. Reuben married Wilma Price. Mary married John Walker.

CHAPTER 176 *Sixth Generation.*

Children of John Bridges and wife, Cinthia Jones· Wilson W married Louisa Hamrick Zecheriah married Nancy Hamrick Louise married Elijah Reuben Hamrick. Susanna married Crawford Hamrick. Marion married Sarah Pannell, second wife, Mary Ann McDaniel Madison married Jane Ramsey second wife, Mary Ann McPhearson Edmond J. married Elizabeth Mitchell Gold; second wife, Mary L Baucom. James Monroe married Martha Beam, second wife Laura Kendall. Albert married Ersley Pricilla Harrell. Thomas married Carrie Reaves second wife Lela Dodd Octavia married Samuel Augustus McKinney. Zulia married William Putnam. Louisa married Martin Green Martha never married.

CHAPTER 177 *Sixth Generation*

Children of Caleb Bridges and wife. Nancy Young: Samuel married Delphia Hardin Martha married Robbin Green Catherine married Eliah Hamrick. Patience married Noah Green Mary married Berry Lovelace Lucindy married Willis Green. Rebecca never married Rachael Ann never married

CHAPTER 178 *Seventh Generation*

Children of Samuel Bridges and wife. Delphia Hardin: James never married. Sarah Elizabeth married Asa Cicero Hamrick.

CHAPTER 179. *Sixth Generation.*

Children of Samuel Bridges and wife. Mary Ann Pinson. Amanda married Jezebell Lovelace

Children of Samuel Bridges and wife Nancy Green: James Franklin married Hessentine Hamrick Charles Monroe married Susanna Buchannan Albert Cicero married Laura Weathers; second wife, Susanna Horne Roxanna married Lafayette Early

Children of William Green and wife. Nancy Green. Hannah married   second husband, Amose Brindell.   Jane married Asa Green.   Willis married Mary Ann Green.   Cleo married Sylvanus Glasgow

CHAPTER 180   *Sixth Generation.*

Children of Robbin Green and wife, Mary Bridges: Noah married Sara Ann Dycus.   Samuel married Narcissus Padgett.   William married Malindy Lovelace.   Mary married George Lovelace.

Children of Robbin Green and wife Martha Bridges.   Junius married ——— Spratt.

CHAPTER 181   *Seventh Generation*

Children of Noah Green and wife Sarah Ann Dycus·   Chauncy married Laura Tessmeer.   Panthia married Ensley Lovelace.   Callie married Martin Ramsey.

CHAPTER 182.   *Seventh Generation.*

Children of William Green and wife, Malindy Lovelace·   Sidney married Dovie Wright   Calvin married Nancy Hatfield.   Edna married Dora Cogdell: second wife, Ollie Jones, third wife, Catherine Bailey.   Dorothy married Robert Butler.   Charles never married.   Marshall Lotian never married.

CHAPTER 183.   *Seventh Generation*

Children of Samuel Green and wife, Narcissus Padgett.   Ellen married James Bright.   Carrie married Smith Bridges   Emeline married Grayson Walker: second husband, Achillis Daves   McKinsey married Nancy Blankinship.   Seth married Georgeanna Bridges. Belvey never married

CHAPTER 184.   *Seventh Generation.*

Children of George Lovelace and wife, Mary Ann Green.   Nolvey married Biddie Hamrick   James married Susanna Blankinship. Joseph L married Ira Wright   Luke married Leckie Wright   Laura Jane marrie ! I: .. \' !   .. \ .l.. .. t l   I: dgers.

8

Genevia married Robert McEntire. Olavine married Guyman Rayburn

CHAPTER 185. *Sixth Generation.*

Children of Louis Sparks and wife, Sarah Bridges Andrew married Martha Sperlin Caleb married Emily Watson Ensley married Mattie Biggerstaff. Landrum married Mary Mintz (no children).

CHAPTER 186. *Seventh Generation*

Children of Andrew Sparks and wife, Martha Sperlin: Caleb married Beula Wall. Sarah married Sidney Jones. Jesse married Lillie Harrell Hessie married Noah Patterson Guffey William married Pearl ————. Fannie not married. Callie never married.

CHAPTER 187. *Seventh Generation.*

Children of Ansley Sparks and wife, Mattie Biggerstaff· Arthur married Maybell Montague John married Floy Hamrick. Thelma married Lassie Byers. Ella married Ezekiel Fowles. Eva married Albert Street Green Lowell married Joseph Martin. Georgie married Garrison Edwards Clarence never married.

CHAPTER 188. *Sixth Generation.*

Children of Calvin Sparks and wife, Susanna Bridges. Jane married John Cartee Mary married Napoleon Boneparte McBrayer. Merritt never married.

CHAPTER 189 *Seventh Generation.*

Children of Napoleon Boneparte McBrayer and wife, Mary Sparks· George married Elizabeth Brooks. Ola married Joseph Owen Thomas Lorenzo married Nancy Culbreth Effie married Bunyan Henderson. Dovie married Volney Ruppe. Bessie married Aden Hamrick. Etta married Grant Allen. James Calvin married Nanzie Brice. John never married Allice not married. Lola not married

Chapter 190. *Sixth Generation.*

Children of Edward Parish Jones and wife, Charlotte Bridges: Joseph Hamilton married Susanna Green. Susanna married Doctor Abram Franklin Hamrick. Biddie married William B. Stroud (no children). Edmond never married. Newton never married James Crowder never married Sarah never married. Jane never married. Alfred Webb never married Drury Dobbins never married.

Chapter 191. *Seventh Generation.*

Children of Joseph Hamilton Jones and wife, Susanna Green: Foster married May Poston. Vider married Monroe Heafner. Clyde married Addie Harrell Joseph not married.

Chapter 192. *Sixth Generation*

Children of Reuben Bridges and wife, Cinthia Harrell. David married Celia Davis; second wife, Ida Philbeck. Jane married Noah Green; second husband, Alonzo Rollins.

Chapter 193. *Sixth Generation*

Children of Washington Bridges and wife, Artie Hamrick: Seaton married Josina McSwain. Wiley married Nancy Susanna Hamrick Thomas married Margarett Hamrick (no children) Charlotte never married.

Chapter 194 *Seventh Generation*

Children of Seaton Bridges and wife, Josina McSwain. Coleman married Marland Jenkins. Gerthie married Boneparte Welman. Ella married William Wright Minnie not married. Arthur not married Newton not married. Carver not married. Oscar never married. Albert never married Collis never married. Annie Bell never married. Ola never married Two infants.

Chapter 195. *Fifth Generation.*

Children of Aaron Bridges and wife, Sarah Hamrick. Drury married Ethie Llwithie Hicks. Timmon married Silveane Jolley

Rosanna married Osborne Lee   Drucindy married Asa Hamrick.
Pricilla married George Lee.

Chapter 196 *Sixth Generation*

Children of Drury Bridges and wife, Ethie Elwithie Hicks   Mary
married Burton Cragg Lovelace.   Aaron A. married Matilda Bridges;
second wife, Alice Justice   Jefferson D. married Lettie Hawkins.
Mattie married Howell Pearson (no children)   Kisiah married
Ray Hollifield   Josie married James Louis Hamrick. Joseph S.
married Bessie Lankfort (no children).   William P. never married.
Maundy never married.   Catherine never married.   Essie never
married.

Chapter 197. *Seventh Generation*

Children of Timmons Bridges and wife, Silveraney Jolley: Kisiah
married John Moore   Ellen married Joseph Beason.   James W.
married Mary Beason.

Chapter 198. *Sixth Generation*

Children of George Lee and wife, Pricilla Bridges: William
Crook married Drucindy Hardin, second wife, Ida Cline.   Franklin
married Sarah London   Phoebia married Cathie Wolfe.   Sarah
married John Walker   Jane married Eli P Shuford   John never
married   Owens never married.

Chapter 199 *Seventh Generation*

Children of William Crook Lee and wife Drucindy Hardin:
George married Carrie London   Franklin married Minnie Rollins.
Blanch married Clarence Clasgow   Jane married Plato Bridges
Emma married George Hord   Robert never married.   Hester never
married

Chapter 200 *Seventh Generation*

Children of John Walker and wife, Sarah Lee· Zecheriah married
Victoria Lovelace; second wife, Lucindy Wall. Laura married John
A Jenk   E beth married Louis Scruggs·   Margaret married

OLD CRACKING REEL USED FOR WOOL OR COTTON MANUFACTURE. (SEE PAGE 27)

Garry Whitaker. Benjamin never married. Foster never married. Carrie never married

CHAPTER 201. *Seventh Generation.*

Children of Cathy Wolfe and wife, Phoebia Lee: William married Mary Wesson. George married Etta Goode. Sanford married Sarah Sellers Florence married Pinkney Lackey. Dewey married Emma McGill. Mary married William Blanton. Jane married William Jenkins. Ellen married Doctor Grigg. Erie never married.

CHAPTER 202. *Seventh Generation.*

Children of Eli P. Shuford and wife, Jane Lee John married Ella Copeland, second wife, Amanda Propes. William married Martha Frances Blanton Robert married Bessie Peeler. George married Eva Crowder. Sarah married Chauncey Hastin Alice married Lawson Davis. Margaret married Franklin Grigg. One infant.

CHAPTER 203. *Sixth Generation.*

Children of Osborne Lee and wife, Rosanna Bridges. Drucindy married Leander Holland. Pricilla married Drury S Lovelace. John married Penina Elmore Drury married Helen Harrell Timmons Gamewell married Permelia Holland Osborne married Edith Blanton.

CHAPTER 204 *Seventh Generation.*

Children of Leander Holland and wife, Drucindy Lee Timmons C married Missouri Bridges. Rosanna married Pinkney Randall. Louisa married George Matheney Osborne W married Eva Jenkins. Austin married Louise Fortune Mary married Gifton Wall Permelia married Thomas Wilkins. Leroy married Flois Hamrick James never married. Games not married.

CHAPTER 205 *Seventh Generation.*

Children of Timmons Gamewell Lee and wife, Permelia Ann Holland: Lawrence Victor married Susanna Lattimore   Etta married Robert Lee Green.

CHAPTER 206   *Seventh Generation*

Children of Drury Lee and wife, Helen Harrell: John married Ida Estella Hamrick. Wesley married Rockaney Hamrick. Charles married Mittie Green. Joseph married Willie Carter. Elizabeth married William Clinton Hamrick. Susanna married Pinkney Hamrick. Sidney married Susanna Pierce.

CHAPTER 207   *Seventh Generation.*

Children of Osborne Lee and wife, Edith Blanton. Elizabeth married Noah Jolley. William never married

CHAPTER 208.   *Seventh Generation.*

Children of John Lee and wife, Penina Elmore   Ellen married Junius Lovelace   Marindy married Benjamin Hughes.

CHAPTER 209   *Seventh Generation.*

Children of John Moore and wife, Kisiah Bridges: Columbus married Ellen Eillson; second wife, Cora Surratt. Dela married Marion Scruggs   Ida married Benjamin Humphries. Eva married Tilman Bridges   William married ——— Webber. Susanna married William Buice. Irvin married Panthia Davis. D. D. married Joseph Humphries. Ollie never married.

CHAPTER 210.   *Seventh Generation.*

Children of Joseph Beason and wife, Ellen Bridges   Grady married Hattie Ramsey. Robert married ———.   Kinsey married Frances Scruggs   Pinkney married Dicie Waters. Clinton married Mary Tate. Paul married Loney Green   Eugenia married Joseph McCraw   Docia married Charles Tate   Perrilla married Rondy Green

CHAPTER 211. *Seventh Generation.*

Children of James W. Bridges and wife, Mary Beason: Chivus married Arkansas Green, second wife, Lottie Hamrick. Rex married Oder McSwain. Zenophan T. married Euzelia McCraw. Cuttie never married.

CHAPTER 212 *Fifth Generation*

Children of John Bridges and wife Elizabeth Bridges. Drury married Elizabeth Robertson. Malindy married Robert Wilson Ephraim married Ella Dobbins. Thomas married Margaret Winbrown. William married Fannie Winbrown Samuel married Mary Winbrown, second wife, Catherine Harrell John S. married Vianna Byers; second wife, Vianna Padgett. Dial married Dennie Scruggs (no children) Berry married Sarah Maze Aaron never married.

CHAPTER 213. *Sixth Generation.*

Children of Drury Bridges and wife, Elizabeth Robertson· Lorenzo married Sarah Wiggins Thomas married Martha Hicks. Beattie married Mary Jane White. George married Amanda Smart Susanna married Julius Melton. Amandy married Emulus Walker Jayson married Mary Good. Adeline married Daniel Peeler. William married Callie Norrells Dora married ———— Hawkins.

CHAPTER 214. *Sixth Generation*

Children of Robert Wilson and wife, Malindy Bridges James married Christine Hawkins Elizabeth married James Rollins Benjamin never married John never married

CHAPTER 215. *Sixth Generation*

Children of Thomas Bridges and wife, Margaret Winbrown Thompson married Patience Durham, second wife, Kisiah Adeline Pearson Samuel married Martha Brown. Charles married Margaret Harris William married Docia Fortune. Landrum married Mary Jenkins John married Hattie Parker. James married Minnie Reel ～ ‥ ‥ married Franklin Blanton. George married

Belle Blanton; second wife, Susanna Hughes. Sarah married Marion Harmon (no children). Clementine never married Dial never married. Martha never married.

CHAPTER 216. *Sixth Generation*

Children of William Bridges and wife, Fannie Winbrown · Monroe married Susanna Bibbie. Hill married Susanna Philbeck. Bankston married Clarenda Ledbetter. Jane married Asbury G. Wiggins. Catherine married Quinn Padgett Lucindy married Lawson Price. Bruce married Lula White. Leah Verge married George Melton. Wade never married. Berry never married

CHAPTER 217. *Sixth Generation*

Children of Samuel Bridges and wife, Mary Winbrown. James married Frances Bibbie. John married Luraney Jones, second wife, Sarah Edwards. Victoria married Jefferson Davis Bridges. Plato married Dora Dycus Lucretia married Alexander McDaniel (no children). William married Elizabeth Bridges. Pinkney married Sarah Hamrick Louisa married Franklin Whisnant. Susanna married Aaron Wall Margaret married Dobbins Hunt Malindy married Joseph Self. Octavia married Taylor Wall.

CHAPTER 218 *Sixth Generation.*

Children of John S. Bridges and wife, Vianna Byers. Monroe married Alice Blanton Sarah married John Wright Nancy married Larkin Green, second husband, Dobbins Robbinson Jane married Richard Wiggins.

Children of John S Bridges and wife, Vianna Padgett Roxanna married Whitstone Blanton. Arkansas married Amose Bridges.

CHAPTER 219 *Sixth Generation.*

Children of Berry Bridges and wife, Sarah Maze Greenberry married Martha Bedford Susanna married Columbus Jolley. Elizabeth married Drury Green; second husband Robert Philbeck.

CHAPTER 220 *Fifth Generation.*

Children of Burwell Blanton and wife, Phoebia Margaret Bridges: Charles married Judia Hamrick Nancy married Joseph Byers, second husband, Abram Padgett George married Pricilla Harrell. Susanna married William Wimbrown. James married Mary Bridges; second wife, Rebecca Hamrick Jesse married Fannie Tate; second wife, Liddie Sapaugh (no children). John married Rebecca Hughes Sarah married Young Hughes. Elizabeth married Thomas Harris.

CHAPTER 221 *Sixth Generation*

Children of Charles Blanton and wife, Judia Hamrick: John married Gatherie Stroud. William married Josephine Setzer. Albert married Roxanna Irvin Jane married Drury Dobbins Suttle. Margaret married Minor Doggett. Elvira married Joseph Suttle Burwell married Frances Doggett; second wife, Martha Ramsey George married Mary Jane Elliott Pinkney never married. Gilford never married James never married.

CHAPTER 222 *Seventh Generation.*

Children of John Blanton and wife, Gatherie Strowd. Ola married Benjamin Hampton Charles William married George Rollins. John Broadus married Ida Biggerstaff Eula married Robert E. Biggerstaff Rudolph married Minnie Fortune. Alda never married Roy not married.

CHAPTER 223 *Seventh Generation.*

Children of Minor Doggett and wife, Margaret Blanton; Charles married Laura Wray Elizabeth married Steady Lipscomb. George married Agnes Halliburton. Florence married James Cowan. Thomas married Bennie Riggs Halliburton married Dora Brown.

CHAPTER 224 *Seventh Generation*

Children of Albert Blanton and wife, Roxanna Irvin. Charles Irvin married Permeha Cabiness. Martha married David Mc-Brayer Joseph married Hester Bott- Permeha married Thomas

Clingman Eskridge. Lawson married John Wray. Beattie not married

CHAPTER 225. *Seventh Generation*

Children of William Blanton and wife, Josephine Setzer: William married Minnie Neal Cephus married Mattie Shuford Dobbins married Nancy Fleming. Albert married Charlotte Walker. Charles never married.

CHAPTER 226. *Seventh Generation.*

Children of Joseph Suttle and wife, Elvira Blanton: Albert Benjamin married Lou Miller Charles Beatty married Esther Wray. Sarah married George Wray. Esther married Dr Victor McBrayer.

CHAPTER 227. *Seventh Generation.*

Children of Drury Dobbins Suttle and wife, Jane Blanton: Donna married Edward Wright Pinkney never married. Emma never married Ella never married Joseph never married Frances never married.

CHAPTER 228. *Seventh Generation.*

Children of Burwell Blanton and wife, Frances Doggett: Charles Coleman married Ora Brewster. Mary married Richard Eskridge. Margaret married George Webb George married Ida Wood. Dora married Rush Oats Edgar Burwell married Mary Martin.

CHAPTER 229. *Sixth Generation*

Children of William Wimbrown and wife, Susanna Blanton: Wallace married Jane Hawkins Mary married Samuel Bridges. Margaret married Thomas Bridges. Fannie married William Bridges. Julia Ann married Ransom Newton Hawkins. Lucretia married Lemuel Pearson Emma married Jacob Smith. Eunice married William Ledbetter Octavia married Henderson Hawkins; second husband, Jefferson Hawkins Sarah married Jefferson Hawkins.

CHAPTER 230 *Seventh Generation.*

Children of Wallace Winn and wife, Jane Hawkins: Orvi married Jane Hawkins. Catherine married Thomas Padgett. Susanna married Achella Padgett. Mary married Ward Padgett. Leuvenia married George Wood. Minervia married John Wilkins. James never married.

CHAPTER 231. *Seventh Generation*

Children of Ransom Newton Hawkins and wife, Julia Ann Winbrown: Governor Vance married Olive Blanton, second wife, Bessie Gladden. Armindy married Burwell B. Blanton. Preston married Susanna Smith. William T married Nancy Blanton. John H. married Hattie Hughes. Joseph married Etta Smith. Callie married George Moore. Dora married Cicero Lovelace. Octavia E. married James L Green. Robert N never married.

CHAPTER 232 *Seventh Generation.*

Children of Reuben Pearson and wife, Lucretia Winbrown: Kisiah Adeline married Thompson Bridges. Caroline married Zenothan Blanton. Luke never married. Hannah never married. Nancy never married. James never married.

CHAPTER 233 *Seventh Generation.*

Children of Lemuel Pearson and wife, Elizabeth Winbrown. Jesse married Mary Blanton. George married Missouri Champion. William married Sarah Blanton. Howell married Chestine Ownes; second wife, Mattie Bridges. Elizabeth married John White. Mattie married John Harrell. Nancy Susanna never married. Catherine never married.

Children of Andy Blanton and wife, Elizabeth Winbrown; John Franklin never married. Judith never married.

CHAPTER 234 *Sixth Generation*

Children of Joseph Byers and wife, Nancy Blanton: Crayton married Lucy Padgett. Burwell Benson married Mary Blanton.

George married Margaret Doggett. Elizabeth married James Bedford; second husband, Wiley Bridges. William never married

CHAPTER 235. *Seventh Generation.*

Children of Crayton Byers and wife. Emeline Philbeck: James married Josephine Runyans. Joseph married Hattie Martin. Martha married Adolphus Hamrick. Laura married John Hamrick. Nancy married Marshall Bowens. Chivus married Georgia Hardin Franklin never married.

CHAPTER 236. *Seventh Generation.*

Children of Burwell Benson Byers and wife, Mary Blanton. Benjamin Franklin married Theodocia Price John James married Roseline Smart; second wife, Ella Ruppe. Joseph Crayton married Drilla Price. Mary married Armbristor Smart. Nancy married John Blanton.

CHAPTER 237 *Seventh Generation.*

Children of George Byers and wife, Margaret Doggett: John married Nancy Gullick. George married Margaret Bridges, second wife Elizabeth Elliott Kansas Ellen married James Young Hamrick. Missouri married Alexander Fergusson. Massie married Aaron Reuben Hamrick. Josephine never married.

CHAPTER 238. *Sixth Generation*

Children of George Blanton and wife, Pricilla Harrell: Beattie married Julia Webb; second wife, Elmira Whitsides Susanna married James Young Margaret married Alexander Wray Pricilla Jane married George Melton Webb. Hill married Amanda Whitsides. Guilford married Mary Johnston

CHAPTER 239. *Seventh Generation.*

Children of James Young and wife, Susanna Blanton. George married Margaret Lorance (no children). Margaret married Dr Oliver P Gardner. Dr Guilford married Florence Jackson. Pri-

cilla married Greenberry Padgett   Sarah Jane married John Quinn
Nancy married Thomas Moore.   Estella married Columbus Martin
Samuel married Elizabeth Manney, second wife, Jane Goode   James
married Julia Ann Gettys. William married Saphronia Wood. Susanna married Isaac Newton Biggerstaff   John never married

CHAPTER 240. *Eighth Generation.*

Children of Dr. Guilford Young and wife, Florence Jackson.
Claude married Claudia Fortune   Olive married Thomas Wilkie
Catherine married Jacob A Alexander   Georgie married Eugene
Brinnerman. Nelle not married   Margaret not married   Belle
never married. Two infants.

CHAPTER 241. *Eighth Generation*

Children of Columbus Martin and wife, Estella Young· Darcus
married Charles Crowell. Mame not married.

CHAPTER 242 *Eighth Generation.*

Children of Dr Oliver P. Gardner and wife, Margaret Young·
Junius T. Gardner married Texanna Noah. Oliver Maxwell married
Fay Lamar Webb   William H married Margaret Wray   Bessie
married Clyde R Hoey   Bate B. married Mary Warren   Addie
married Robert M. Farthing. Cleo married Thomas A. Robertson.
Olive married J Austin Anthony

CHAPTER 243. *Eighth Generation.*

Children of Greenberry Padgett and wife Pricilla Young. Marshall married Mary Welhouser. William married Eric Huntley
Tilden married Cleo King. Maudie married Charles Busbey   Margaret married John Carpenter. Susanna married Wade Tillison
Hague not married.

CHAPTER 244 *Eighth Generation.*

Children of Samuel Young and wife, Elizabeth Manney: Blanch
married Clendan Burns. Cutrie married Joseph Biggerstaff.

OLD-FASHIONED WEAVING LOOM. (SEE PAGE 27)

CHAPTER 245. *Eighth Generation.*

Children of John Quinn and wife, Sarah Jane Young: John W. married Sarah Moss Thomas H married Sarah Hallman Nancy S. married Jacob A. Beam Mary married John Henderson, second husband, Sidney Setzer. Elizabeth married Thomas Whitter. Louisa married John A. Miller.

CHAPTER 246. *Eighth Generation*

Children of James Young and wife, Julia Ann Gettys: Clarence married Esther Taylor. Grady married Lucy Whilhouser. Milus married Pearl Carswell. Elizabeth married Joseph Hardin. Addie married Alster Bedford Clyde never married Cleo not married. Susanna not married. William James not married. Leander not married.

CHAPTER 247 *Eighth Generation*

Children of William Young and wife, Saphronia Wood. Jesse married Clara Blankenship. Margaret married Butler Higgins. Arthur married Effie Flack Gathia married Solon Scoggins Jordan married Bessie Hartell. Two infants.

CHAPTER 248 *Sixth Generation*

Children of James Blanton and wife, Mary Bridges. William Asbury married Lucindy Lovelace
Children of James Blanton and wife, Rebecca Hamrick Drury Allen married Julia Ann Ledbetter. James Hamrick married Catherine Ledbetter. George never married

CHAPTER 249 *Seventh Generation.*

Children of William Asbury Blanton and wife, Lucindy Lovelace· James married Elizabeth Blanton William married Fannie Louisa Smith Elizabeth Jane married Franklin Blanton Miller never married T........ .... married

CHAPTER 250. *Seventh Generation.*

Children of Drury Allen Blanton and wife, Julia Ann Ledbetter.
James Henry married Mary Luvenia Lee. William Norman married Rebecca Blanton. John Summey married Jane Blanton. Burwell Benjamin married Permelia Hawkins. Cordelia Arvezenia married Cicero Hughes. Nancy Jane married Leonard Yelton. Mary Elizabeth married Amos Davis. Julia Ann married Robert A. Houser. Drury Allen never married.

CHAPTER 251. *Sixth Generation*

Children of John Blanton and wife, Rebecca Hughes: Franklin married Sarah Chitwood. William married Emiline Hughes. Andy married Elizabeth Jolley. Mary married Burwell Benson Byers. Rebecca married Doctor Jolley. John married Sarah Hughes. Malindy never married. Albert never married.

CHAPTER 252 *Seventh Generation.*

Children of Franklin Blanton and wife, Sarah Chitwood. John married Martha Hamrick. Jesse married Lora Bridges. Albert married Mary McKey. Julia married Oliver Abram Hamrick. Ellen married Doctor A Price. Sarah married James Louis Hamrick. Malindy married Vernon Allen. Elizabeth married Newton Daves. Fannie married Martin Gold. Eliza married Twitty Daves. James never married. William never married.

CHAPTER 253. *Seventh Generation.*

Children of William Blanton and wife, Emiline Hughes: John married Rosanna Bates. Narcissus married Burwell William Blanton. Greenberry married Nancy Susanna Pearson. Franklin married Lottie Jolley. Julia married James Hamrick. Mollie married Alanson Williams. Elizabeth married George Kelley. Martha not married.

CHAPTER 254 *Seventh Generation.*

Children of Andy Blanton and wife, Elizabeth Jolley. Albert

married Catherine Green   Caroline married Asa Hamrick.   Edith Ellen married Osborne Lee   Mary Missalancy married Jesse Pearson   Nancy Susanna married George Lookado Pruett.   Elizabeth Josephine married Pinkney Bridges.   Jane married Eli Turner. Roxanna married Arthur Blanton.   Crowell never married.

CHAPTER 255 *Seventh Generation*

Children of John Blanton and wife, Sarah Hughes.   Elizabeth married Marcus Morehead   Malindy married William Blanton. Tucker married Jane Blanton.   Jesse never married

CHAPTER 256 *Sixth Generation*

Children of Young Hughes and wife, Sarah Blanton: Putnam married Julia Wray.   Susanna married James McMurry   Amos married Jane Alexander.   Wesley married Sarah Ann Roberts. Elizabeth married Wesley Blanton   Artie Elizabeth married Napoleon Davis.   Narcissus married William Hamrick.   Sarah married John Blanton.   Richard married Elizabeth Hamrick   Jesse never married   Jolley never married.

CHAPTER 257. *Seventh Generation.*

Children of James McMurry and wife, Susanna Hughes: John married Mary White; second wife, Eunice Doty.   James married Mary Dycus   Noah married Minnie Putnam   Julius married Alice Putnam.   Sarah married Crockett Wilson   Nancy married Elijah Dycus   Martha married Samuel Sherrill   Burwell never married Graham never married   Elizabeth never married.   Mary never married.   Susanna never married   Rachael never married   Margaret never married

CHAPTER 258 *Seventh Generation.*

Children of Napoleon Davis and wife, Artie Elizabeth Hughes· Amos married Mary Blanton.   Perry married Permelia Burgin Henry married Savannah Brannan   Leuvenia married Mills Flack. Lenora never married

CHAPTER 259. *Sixth Generation.*

Children of Thomas Harris and wife, Elizabeth Blanton· Burwell married Tegmira Bridges Margaret married James Huskey Emeline married Bowen Bridges

CHAPTER 260 *Seventh Generation*

Children of Bowen Bridges and wife, Emeline Harris: Burton H. married Meldonia McKinney. Margaret B married George Byers. Sarah B married Hartwell Blanton. Thomas Aaron married Mary McSwain. Matilda married Aaron A. Bridges. Thompson married Julia Wood James O. married Elizabeth Roberts Pinkney married Josie Blanton. Susanna never married.

CHAPTER 261. *Seventh Generation.*

Children of Burwell Harris and wife, Tegmira Bridges· John married Carrie Simmons Thomas married Octavia Wiseman Catherine married John Wesley Harrell Ellen married Silas Bland. Emeline married Charles Bridges.

CHAPTER 262. *Seventh Generation.*

Children of James Huskey and wife, Margaret Harris· John married Alice Camp. Thomas married Cordelia Moore. Alexander married Sugar Davis. Julia married Pinkney Scruggs Sarah married Jackson Jones. Mary married William Humphries. Elizabeth married Asbury McCraw. Jenkins married Hattie Hopper. Barney married Prairie Scruggs, second wife, Bessie Ellis. Joel married Zora Scruggs. Albert never married

CHAPTER 263 *Seventh Generation.*

Children of Beattie Blanton and wife, Julia Webb. Hackett married Dela Hamrick. John married Orelia Barr; second wife, Mary Persall.

CHAPTER 264   *Seventh Generation*

Children of Hill Blanton and wife, Amanda Whitsides: Hill married Ida Kendrick. Dovie married John Herndon.

CHAPTER 265   *Seventh Generation.*

Children of George Melton Webb and wife, Pricilla Jane Blanton James Landrum married Arkansas Andrews Edwin Yates married Willie Simmons. George married Margaret Blanton. Charles married Ida Cox. Dora married Summey Alexander. Edna married John Darwin.

CHAPTER 266   *Seventh Generation.*

Children of Alexander Wray and wife, Margaret Blanton: George married Sarah Suttle Pricilla married James Toms James L. married Amanda Hogue Julius married Susanna Toms. Arthur married Ellen Dameron. Esther married Charles Beattie Suttle Docia married William H. Jennings Emmulus married Alice Amelia Dennis; second wife, Susanna Chapman

CHAPTER 267.   *Fifth Generation.*

Children of Henry Ledbetter and wife, Vianna Bridges. Elijah married Rebecca Jones Anonymus married Permelia McSwain; second wife, Rebecca McSwain Eurias married Nancy Bridges. William married Eunice Winbrown Saleny married Robert Champion Elmira married James Hughes. Arriemia married William McSwain Julia married Drury Allen Blanton. Catherine married James Hamrick Blanton Sylvira married William Hamrick (no children). Frankie married Marcus McSwain.

CHAPTER 268   *Sixth Generation.*

Children of Elijah Ledbetter and wife, Rebecca Jones· William married Julia McDaniel. Elijah married Narcissus Earl. Susanna married Reuben McSwain Jane married James David Green. Elizabeth married William Robbins·

CHAPTER 269. *Sixth Generation.*

Children of Anonymus Ledbetter and wife, Rebecca McSwain:
Smith married Nancy Ann Blanton.

CHAPTER 270. *Sixth Generation.*

Children of Eurias Ledbetter and wife, Nancy Bridges: John
married Mary Lee; second wife, Mary Flack. Columbus M. married
Priscilla Smith. Cleophus married Anonymus McSwain.

CHAPTER 271. *Sixth Generation.*

Children of Robbin Champion and wife, Saleny Ledbetter: George
married Mary Jane Hamrick; second wife, Sarah Hamrick; third
wife, Susanna Putnam. James married Jane Turner. Sarah married William Hamrick (no children) Martha married Thomas Mc-
Swain. Mary married George Pearson Caroline married James
Blanton Lucretia married Elam Weaver. Stansberry married
Samanthy Padgett Crowell never married.

CHAPTER 272 *Fifth Generation.*

Children of Benjamin Hughes and wife, Nancy Bridges. James
married Elmira Ledbetter Sarah married Jesse Jolley Nancy
married James Hicks Mary married Thomas Pruett (no children);
second husband, Asa Hamrick (no children). Elizabeth married
Burwell Hamrick, second husband, Willis Hicks. William married
Rebecca Justice Sanford married Verdie Durham. Starland married Nancy Hamrick.

CHAPTER 273 *Sixth Generation.*

Children of Jesse Jolley and wife, Sarah Hughes. James Porch
married Malindy Moore. Willis married Susanna Bridges. Asbury
married Sarah Moore. Jesse Landrum married Cinthia McBraver
(no children). Crawford married Lucretia Jolley Amose married
Sarah Lovelace. Irene married Thompson Barnett. Kisiah Emiline
married Berry Hawkins Sarah Malindy married James Crowder

Pruett Jane married James Hamrick Susanna married Thomas Hamrick. Cynthia Carolina never married Elizabeth Airenia never married. Lucindy never married.

Chapter 274. *Sixth Generation.*

Children of James Hicks and wife, Nancy Hughes· Gather married Susanna Goforth.

Chapter 275 *Sixth Generation*

Children of William Hughes and wife, Rebecca Justice Doctor married Mary Davis. Amanda married James David Barnett. Julia married Robert Davis Drury married Mary Jane Davis (no children). Annettie married William Ferrell. Mary married Evans Chitwod. Joseph never married Laura never married Nancy never married. Four infants

Chapter 276 *Sixth Generation.*

Children of Sanford Hughes and wife, Virdie Dunham. David married Mary Beam Jackson married Martha Gold. Almernay married Miles Francis Veranda married Doctor S. Putnam Jane married Cleophus Ellis. Sanford married Mary Jane McEntire Green married Cinthia Tate. Benjamin married Malindy Jolley. Richard married Eliza Turner, second wife, Elizabeth Goode. Sarah-ann married John Turner Harriett married Wade Blanton.

Chapter 277. *Sixth Generation*

Children of David Dunham and wife Malindy Hughes· Seaton Gales never married. Noah married Essie Coleman. Hill married Mary Sullivan John married Sarah Shuford; second wife, Malindy Lewis. Jane married Rease Davis. Benjamin never married. Verandy never married Cora never married

Chapter 278 *Sixth Generation*

Children of Burwell Bridges and wife, Nancy Elizabeth Harman· Walter married Sarah Blanton. Andrew married Sarah Lee.

Amanda married Adolphus Roberts. Nancy married Enrids Ledbetter Wallace never married Pinkney never married. Franklin
never married Burwell never married

CHAPTER 279. *Fifth Generation.*

Children of James Bridges and wife, Elizabeth Hamrick. Wiley
married Vianna Huckeby, second wife, Elizabeth Byers (no children) Anderson married Nancy Bedford James married Biddie
Johnston, second wife, Mary Gold. Mary married Joseph Bedford
(no children) Elizabeth married John Beam (no children).
Frankie married Rodney Doggett (no children). Mary never married.

CHAPTER 280. *Sixth Generation*

Children of James Bridges and wife, Biddie Johnston: Jefferson
Davis married Victoria Bridges. Elizabeth married John Wamac.
Ellen married George Goforth Octavia married Benjamin Wall.
James married Attie Davis, second wife, Susanna Murk. William
married Louisa McFarland. Wiley never married. Willis never
married

CHAPTER 281. *Sixth Generation.*

Children of Anderson Bridges and wife, Nancy Bedford. Eliza-
beth married William Bridges. Martha married Berry Wall Mar-
garet married Jesse Harrell Airie married John Teeter Wilson
Susanna married Robert Lee McDaniel. Laura married Amose
Bridges Florence married Valentine Whitaker. Fannie married
Craton McDaniel

CHAPTER 282 *Fifth Generation.*

Children of William Bridges and wife, Elizabeth Bridges. Ezekiel
married Permelia Webb Cameron married Susanna Bowens. James
married Marthian Dycus Sarah married James Jones. Elizabeth
married William Connor. Mary married Jesse Doty. Artie married

Jesse Hardin (no children). Yates never married. Mariah never married. Margaret never married. Nancy never married.

Chapter 283 *Sixth Generation*

Children of Ezekiel Bridges and wife, Permelia Webb· Lawson A. married Mary Justice. William married Mary Ann Walker Alfred married Susanna Wright. Amos married Parmelia Robertson; second wife, Jocansas Bridges David married Margaret Horton. Wiley married Eva McCall Celia married William Wright; second husband, Green Dycus Arbella married Hamby Davis Isaac James married Lanedsey Dicus. John never married. Dial never married. Burwell never married.

Chapter 284 *Seventh Generation*

Children of Lawson A Bridges and wife, Mary Justice: Columbus married Nancy Blanton Dawson married Blanch Wright. Etta married James Green Josie married Marcus Stockton Georgia married Robert Gold.

Chapter 285 *Seventh Generation.*

Children of Alfred Bridges and wife, Susanna Wright. Bryson married Etta Jones, second wife, Mary Ellen Price. Malindy married Willis Webb Green married Nancy Price George married Sophia Ownes Joseph B married Elmira Grigg Nancy married Noah Lovelace.

Chapter 286 *Seventh Generation*

Children of William Bridges and wife, Mary Ann Walker: Summey married Ester Williams Jane married Otus Carson Malissa married Andy Price. Crowell married Mary Hardin Plato married Jane Lee. James married Ella Abernathy. Alonzo married Etta Robbins Frances married George Floyd. Hester married Willis Hoyle Ella married Chaney Price

CHAPTER 287. *Seventh Generation*

Children of David Bridges and wife, Margaret Horton: George Miller never married. Biddie not married.

CHAPTER 288 *Seventh Generation*

Children of William Wright and wife, Celia Bridges: George married Sarah Ann Dycus Lawson married Jane Allen; second wife, Jane Ruppe. Frankie married Daniel Philbeck. Hester married Thomas Doty. Isabell married James Culbreth. Emeline never married

Children of Green Dycas and wife, Celia Bridges· Riccy married Willis Owens. Biddie married Huston Pool. Rosanna married Drury Dobbins Webb. Carrie married Duffie Spratt. William married Johnnie Cogdell. James married Georgia Bailey. Julianne never married.

CHAPTER 289. *Seventh Generation.*

Children of Isaac James Bridges and wife, Louisa Dycas· Joseph D married Ella Price. Zecheriah married Caroline Ramsey. Dond married William Pinkney McKinney. Mincey married Andy Price Amanda not married

CHAPTER 290. *Sixth Generation.*

Children of James Bridges and wife, Martha Dycas: George married Texana Wells. Neeley married Roseline Philbeck Kimsey married Liddie Felker. Newton married Josie Felker Clayton married Samanthia Hesentine Brooks, second wife, Missouri Felker. Joseph Married Lenora Horne Elizabeth married James Fowler Roseline married Landrum White. Texanna married John Morgan John married Susanna Wiggins. Leander never married.

CHAPTER 291 *Fifth Generation*

Children of Wiley Bridges and wife, Eva McColl. Carrie married Harvey Vinson Claud married ——— ———. Ralph married ——— ———. Pearl married Fredrick Nixon Earl never married Maudie never married Edna never married. Franklin never married Clay never married. Daulton not married.

Chapter 292 *Fifth Generation*

Children of Jesse Doty and wife, Mary Bridges Osborne never married

Chapter 293 *Seventh Generation.*

Children of Hamby Davis and wife, Arbella Bridges· Joseph married Margaret White, second wife, Priscilla Jane Jones Hill married Frances Philbeck Melton Webb married Maryann Wright. Dexton married Mamie Stockton: second wife, Mary McCurry. Simon married Eva Whitesides Essie married Thomas Bostic. Louisa married John Grayson Permelia married John Melton.

Chapter 294 *Sixth Generation*

Children of William Conner and wife, Elizabeth Bridges· Franklin married Maryann Spanglar, second wife, Caroline Hawkins Hoyle married Martha Philbeck. Mary Jane married Edman Glascoe William never married. Alber never married.

Chapter 295 *Seventh Generation*

Children of Edmon Glascoe and wife, Mary Jane Conner: Margaret Lucindy married Avery Smith. William E. married Octavia Grigg Doctor John married Ola Bridges; second wife, Cora Street. Carrie May married Landreth McSwain Martha Jane married Alexander Wilson Minnie Olive married James L Spanglar. Carrie Lavenia never married.

Chapter 296. *Seventh Generation*

Children of Franklin Conner and wife, Maryann Spanglar· Jane married Albert Horne Cleo married William Tessaneer. Essie married Stonewall Manney Ossie married William Weathers. Zoar married Hugh Champion Two infants

CHAPTER 297. *Seventh Generation.*

Children of Hoyle Connar and wife, Martha Philbeck. Cora married David Francis. Nitia married Boss Green. James married Eunice Willis. Mary married William Green. Alonzo married Lenard Gocey. Bertie married John Murphy

CHAPTER 298 *Sixth Generation*

Children of James Jones and wife, Sarah Bridges: David Dial married Mary Collins; second wife Emily Susanna Jones. Starline married Malindy Philbeck. John married Susanna Jones. Perry never married. Martha Jane never married. Mariah never married. James Wiley never married Mary never married Wilson never married

CHAPTER 299. *Seventh Generation*

Children of David Dial Jones and wife, Mary Collins· James married Catherine Nelson, second wife Eliza Jane Bennett. Wilson married ———— Williams. Asberry married Jane Haynes. Mary married Angus Fortenberry. Willis never married.

Children of David Dial Jones and wife, Emily Susanna Jones Doctor Seaton married Hilda Jane Jones. Leander Jasper married Lillie Collis. Sarah Loucindy married Berry Lemons. Fannie Eugenia married John Grant. Perry Alexander never married.

CHAPTER 300. *Seventh Generation.*

Children of Starlin Jones and wife, Malindy Philbeck Amos Wall married Martha Burton William Columbus married Martha Humphries Asberry B married Malindy Jenkins Emeline married Bryson Bridges. Elizabeth married David Tate. Etta married Joseph White. Martha Gold never married

CHAPTER 301. *Seventh Generation.*

Children of John Jones and wife, Susanna Jones. Nancy married James Holland.

CHAPTER 302   *Fifth Generation.*

Children of George Bridges and wife, Mary Matheney. David married Elizabeth McSwain. William married Mary McSwain. Hassell married Adlissey Hicks, second wife, Mahaley Hord Abrian married Mary Allen Lawson married Emeline McSwain Vianna married Crawford White, (no children). Frankie married Carney Huffstettler. Mary married James McSwain. Elizabeth married Lee Kendrick. Sarah never married

CHAPTER 303   *Sixth Generation.*

Children of Lawson Bridges and wife, Emeline McSwain: Herriott married Thomas Camp. Ellen married James Saunders. Martha never married

CHAPTER 304   *Sixth Generation*

Children of Hassell Bridges and wife, Adalissey Hicks Fletcher married Hester Roberts. Permelia married Miller Rudasill. Toliver Rush never married.

CHAPTER 305.   *Sixth Generation.*

Children of Abrian Bridges and wife, Mary Allen· Samantha never married. Liddie married ———— Batie.

CHAPTER 306.   *Sixth Generation*

Children of Crawford White and wife, Vianna Bridges. William married ———— Ross Georgie never married. Mary never married One infant.

CHAPTER 307   *Fourth Generation.*

Children of William McSwain and wife, Susanna Hamrick· William married Judith Moore David married Rebecca Cowart, second wife. Catherine Robertson Benjamin married Rebecca Smith Priscilla married Gabriel Washburn Jonathan married Sarah Norwood Elizabeth married John Matheney. Charles mar-

OLD TYPE OF WINDING BLADES USED IN THE MANUFACTURE OF COTTON AND WOOLEN GOODS. (SEE PAGE 28)

ried Margaret Norwood. James married Elizabeth Moore (no children).

CHAPTER 308. *Fifth Generation.*

Children of William McSwain and wife Judith Moore David married Susanna Hamrick James married Sarah Bostic Hannah married Ruben Hamrick. Sarah married David Hamrick Mary married Elijah Hamrick Rebecca married George Champion Elizabeth married James Moore. William married Mary Bridges. John married Judith Moore. Judith married John Green. Thomas married Frankie Bridges George married Mary Weathers. Susanna never married.

CHAPTER 309 *Sixth Generation.*

Children of John McSwain and wife, Judith Moore: Louis married Mary Hamrick. Martha married William Hamrick, second husband, George Hardin Judith married David Moore. Nancy married Wiley Padget.

CHAPTER 310. *Seventh Generation*

Children of Louis McSwain and wife, Mary Hamrick· Reuben married Judith Margaret McSwain; second wife. Susanna Ledbetter Nancy married Abram Hamrick. Hannah married James Moore Green. Judith married Edmond Padgett Elizabeth married Elijah Hamrick Bonnar married Nancy Bird John married Eliza Hardin. Lucey married Jonathan Love Louis Moore married Sarah Roberts Sarah married Christopher Stewart Martha married Posey Hopper. Ambrose married Emeline Hamrick. Margaret married Thomas Hamrick Harvey never married

CHAPTER 311 *Fifth Generation*

Children of David McSwain and wife. Susanna Hamrick: David married Lucindy McSwain William married Judith Hamrick. Samuel married Mary Lovelace John married Sarah Hamrick; second w᎒ ᎒᎒᎒᎒᎒ ᎒᎒᎒᎒ ᎒᎒᎒᎒ ᎒᎒᎒᎒᎒ H ᎒ : fourth wife, Earsley Daily. George married Lucindy Wright. Berry married Barbara Padgett. Drury married Elizabeth Walker, (no children) Judith married Thomas Lovelace. Jane married Nathaniel Lovelace. Cinthia married Housand Harrell, second husband, Reuben Bridges. Mary married Charles Bostic.

CHAPTER 312 *Sixth Generation*

Children of William McSwain and wife, Judith Hamrick: Elijah married Susanna Hamrick. Mary married William Lovelace. George married Hannah Hamrick. David married Delphia Street Harrell. Judith Margaret married Reuben McSwain. Sarah married James Louis Hamrick. Berryman never married. Ensley never married.

CHAPTER 313. *Seventh Generation.*

Children of Elijah McSwain and wife, Susanna Hamrick: Barnett married Zudie Bostic; second wife, Susanna Hamrick. Achella married Nancy Catherine McSwain. Ella married Drury Dobbins Jones

CHAPTER 314. *Seventh Generation.*

Children of Reuben McSwain and wife, Judith Margaret McSwain: Ensley married Louella Dowdle; second wife, Maggie Gettys. Elijah married Ella Humphries. Mary Judith never married. Berry Cleophas never married. Panthia not married. One infant.

Children of Reuben McSwain and wife, Susanna Ledbetter. Louis Austin married Missouri Putnam. Broadus Bonnar married Crausbey Green. Alpha Amega married Virgil Weaver.

CHAPTER 315. *Seventh Generation*

Children of George McSwain and wife, Hannah Hamrick. George Pinkney never married. Andrew Hamrick never married.

CHAPTER 316. *Seventh Generation.*

Children of David McSwain and wife, Delphia Street Harrell:
John Leonard married Jane Brooks   Vernetia never married.

CHAPTER 317. *Sixth Generation.*

Children of Samuel McSwain and wife, Mary Lovelace· Samuel
married Nancy Ann Hopper, (no children).   Asa A. married Elizabeth Cornwell   Lucindy married Zecheriah R McKinney.

CHAPTER 318. *Eighth Generation.*

Children of Zecheriah R. McKinney and wife, Lucindy McSwain:
Meldonia married Burton H Bridges

CHAPTER 319   *Seventh Generation.*

Children of John McSwain and wife, Sarah Hamrick: Edmon J.
married Edith Bostic; second wife Jesse Murry   Eunice Jane married James McSwain, second husband, Elbert Hughes.

CHAPTER 320   *Eighth Generation.*

Children of Asa A McSwain and wife, Elizabeth Cornwell:
Malery Andrews married Ella Cornwell; second wife, Mollie Corn-
well.   Mollie married Boneparte Smith. (Plato married Dovie
Hamrick.   Joseph never married.   Monroe never married

CHAPTER 321. *Seventh Generation.*

Children of Berry McSwain and wife, Barbara Padgett: Coach
Henderson married Susanna Elliott.   Larkin Arkansas married
Louisa Lovelace.   William Berry married Mary Justice   Drury
Reuben married Willer Ramsey   Cheleedonia married Leander
Padgett   Lucindy married John Davis McSwain; second husband,
John Green.   Barbara Finnettie married William Thomas D Green.
Cordelia married David Christopher Hamrick.

CHAPTER 322   *Seventh Generation*

Children of David McSwain and wife, Lucindy McSwain. Wilham Boswell married Priscilla Weathers   George Champion married Susanna Hamrick.   Susanna married William Thomas Green. Sarah married John Green   James married Eunice Jane McSwain Landrum never married.   Elizabeth never married

CHAPTER 323. *Seventh Generation*

Children of George McSwain and wife, Lucindy Wright: John David married Lucindy McSwain, second wife, Malindy Harriot Padgett   George married Narcissus Hamrick.   William Berry married Millie Ledford   Margaret married Berry Bostic Melton Sarah married Andy Hamrick, second husband, Nimrod Champion.   Cinthia married John Green.   Mary married Hoyle R. Blanton.   Nancy Jane never married.

CHAPTER 324. *Seventh Generation.*

Children of Thomas Lovelace and wife, Judith McSwain: Crawford married Martha Beam.   Eunice married Smith Wilkins

CHAPTER 325 *Seventh Generation*

Children of Charles Bostic and wife, Mary McSwain: David married Amanda Padgett, (no children).   Chesley married Nancy Susanna Hamrick   Susanna married William Wright, (no children).   Eunice married William Wright.   James married Harriett Gardner.   Cinthia never married.   Sarah never married.

CHAPTER 326. *Seventh Generation.*

Children of Housand Harrell and wife, Cinthia McSwain. Dice Elizabeth married Columbus M. Melton, second husband, Rhodes Glover.

CHAPTER 327 *Sixth Generation*

Children of James McSwain and wife, Sarah Bostic. Lucindy married David McSwain.

CHAPTER 328. *Fifth Generation.*

Children of James McSwain and wife, Elizabeth McSwain. David married Judith McSwain   Rebecca married Green Lovelace   Martha married Thomas Green   Sarah married Leander Green   Judith married Stephen Green   Elizabeth married Henry Champion. Malindy married James Porch Jolley.   Mary married Asbury Jolley. Hannah married Berry Hicks.   Eunice married John McSwain. James Married Jane Bridgers   George married Mary McSwain

Chapter 329. *Sixth Generation*

Children of Green Lovelace and wife, Rebecca Moore· Benjamin married Eunice Green.   Albert married Margaret Bradley. Leander married Elizabeth Lovelace   John married Vianna Campbell. Grayson married Mary Campbell.   William married Sarah Bridges.

Chapter 330. *Sixth Generation.*

Children of Thomas Green and wife, Martha Moore. David married Julia Rollins   Elizabeth married James Champion   Rebecca Jane married Richard Champion.   Jane married Ezra Roberts Martha married Miles Francis   Susanna married Walter Wood. Narcissus never married   Sarah never married   Mary never married.

Chapter 331. *Sixth Generation.*

Children of Leander Green and wife, Sarah Moore   James married Mary Wilson, second wife, Hannah Matheney.   Elizabeth married John Burgess.

Chapter 332   *Sixth Generation*

Children of Stephen Green and wife, Judith Moore   Dobbins married Priscilla Blanton; second wife, ———— Webb. Abram married Rebecca Green   Sarah married William Wilson. Elizabeth married George Blanton. George married Margaret Moore   William married Matilda Dobbins.   James married ———— ————. John married ———— ————.

Chapter 333. *Sixth Generation*

Ch   H   ·   · 1   · · ·   1   ·· · Moore   David

married Darthia Phillips; second wife, Jane Patterson   James
married Elizabeth Green   Richard married Rebecca Moore   Narcissus married William Curtice.

CHAPTER 334   *Sixth Generation*

Children of James Porch Jolley and wife, Malindy Moore: Richard married Malissa Green. Sarah married Henry Bedsan   Mary
married Luther Robertson.   George married Julia Rebertson
Eunice never married

CHAPTER 335   *Sixth Generation*

Children of Asbury Jolley and wife, Mary Moore   Edley married
Jane Green. Sarah Ann never married. Margaret never married.

CHAPTER 336.   *Sixth Generation.*

Children of Berry Hicks and wife, Hannah Moore. William Andrew married Cordelia Green.   Willis G. married Nancy Webb
Catherine never married

CHAPTER 337   *Sixth Generation.*

Children of David Oliver Moore and wife, Judith McSwain:
Martha Susanna married Richard McSwain. Sarah Malinda
married Monroe Morgan.   Eunice Jane married Butler Gladden.
Hannah Caroline married Alonzo Hartis.   John James Married
Harriett Roberts; second wife, Hester Campbell. David Hamrick
married Malindy Green. Margaret Ellen never married.

CHAPTER 338.   *Sixth Generation.*

Children of James Moore and wife, Jane Bridges. Auston married Malinda Goode. James Robert married Mary Green. Burwell
married Eliza Scruggs.

CHAPTER 339.   *Fifth Generation.*

Children of William McSwain and wife Mary Bridges. Burwell
married Eliza McSwain second wife Jane Hamrick no children)

THREE TYPES OF EARLY CORN AND WHEAT MILLS.   (SEE PAGE 22)

William married Sarah McSwain. George married Hannah Mc-
Swain. Mary married James Hamrick. Susannah married Allen
Hamrick. Richard married Mary Weathers; second wife, Susanna
Moore. Elizabeth married David Bridges. Nina married Wiley
Padgett. Jane married Benjamin Green.

CHAPTER 340. *Sixth Generation.*

Children of George McSwain and wife, Hannah McSwain. Green
married Margaret McSwain. Thomas married Martha Champion.
Kina married Frankey Ledbetter. Wellington married —— ——.

CHAPTER 341. *Sixth Generation.*

Children of Richard McSwain and wife, Mary Weathers. George
married Mary Hopper. Wallace married Catherine Weathers. Mary
married George Moore. Franklin never married. Albert never
married. Elizabeth never married.

Children of Richard McSwain and wife, Susanna Moore. Alice
Miscellany married Perry Humphries. David Oliver married Alice
McSwain.

CHAPTER 342. *Sixth Generation.*

Children of David Bridges and wife, Elizabeth Moore. William
Philando married Sarah Cism. George married Oldvine Cism. Asberry married Delia Hudson. John never married. Roseline never
married. Cordelia never married. Martha Roseanna never married.

CHAPTER 343. *Sixth Generation.*

Children of Burwell McSwain and wife, Eliza McSwain: Doctor
F. married Margaret Holland. Cinthia married Andrew J. Tate.
Jane married George Davis.

CHAPTER 344. *Fifth Generation*

Children of Thomas McSwain and wife, Frankey Bridges. William married Malissa Gipson, (no children). Thomas married Nancy
Byers. Permelia married Anonymous Ledbetter; second husband,

Starlin Weaver (no children. Eliza married Burwell McSwain. Sarah married William McSwain Hannah married George McSwain. Elizabeth married Hugh Roberts. Judith married Abner Allen Rebecca married Anaymus Ledbetter Mary married William Bridges Prairie married Dulcina McSwain.

CHAPTER 345 *Sixth Generation.*

Children of William McSwain and wife, Arrenia Ledbetter: Thomas married Rebecca Hamrick. Anonymus married Cleophus Ledbetter. Josina married Seaton Bridges. Henry married Harriott Weaver Isabell married Timmons McSwain. Salena married Caphus Lee Frankie never married Vianna married William Cleary

CHAPTER 346

Children of Thomas McSwain and wife, Nancy Byers Monroe married Hannah Hamrick Sarah married Samuel Hogue. Susanna never married.

Children of Thomas McSwain and wife, Mary Bridges: Jane married John Mayes. Allis married Ruphus Allen.

CHAPTER 347. *Sixth Generation*

Children of William Bridges and wife, Mary McSwain David married Jane Bookout; second wife, Margaret Head James married Mary Jane Gantt. Burwell married Martha Goforth William married Sarah McKee. Albert married Mattie McKee. Landrum married Elizabeth Burton Calvin married Canzadie Foster Lawson married Christinia Foster George married Martha Elizabeth Weir Elizabeth never married

CHAPTER 348. *Sixth Generation.*

Children of William McSwain and wife, Sarah McSwain· Perdrie married Dulcenia McSwain. Timmons married Isabell McSwain William married Maggie McSwain. Louisa married ——— ——— Green Robert never married

CHAPTER 349. *Sixth Generation.*

Children of Abner Allen and wife, Judith McSwain. Dixon married Minty Dawson Roxanna married Columbus Camp Walter married Elmira Huffstetler Ruphus married Allis McSwain Elizabeth never married.

CHAPTER 350. *Fifth Generation*

Children of John Green and wife, Judith Green: George married Nancy McSwain; second wife, Patience Washburn William married Matilda Bridges. David married Nancy Hamrick. John married Sarah McSwain. Thomas married Susanna Bridges. Joseph married Sarah Hamrick. James married Priscilla McBrayer, second wife, Sarah Beam Judith married Ruben Green. Mary married Asa Lovelace. Eunice married Harvey Randall. Nancy married Benjamin Franklin McSwain.

CHAPTER 351. *Sixth Generation.*

Children of George Green and wife, Nancy McSwain. Franklin married Wilmina Cabness. Clarrisa married McClain Pannell; second husband, James Green.

Children of George Green and wife, Patience Washburn: Mary Jane married James Robert Moore. Nancy Victoria married Preston McAfee Charles not married. Jefferson not married.

CHAPTER 352. *Sixth Generation.*

Children of David Green and wife, Nancy Hamrick. John married Jane Simmons Judith married James Moore. Elizabeth married Byard Ruppe.

CHAPTER 353. *Sixth Generation.*

Children of John Green and wife, Sarah McSwain. Clemmie married Margaret Champion. William David Fulton married Mollie Stockton. Louandy married James Weaver. Susanna married Cornelius Sanders. Maryann married Thomas Spangler.

Thomas Engenia married Oliver Glasgoe. Patience married Richard Spangler. George never married. Joseph Suttle never married. James McSwain married Missouri Stockton.

Chapter 354. *Sixth Generation*

Children of Thomas Green and wife, Susanna Bridges: Gallener married Elijah Bly Hamrick. Matilda married Wiley Hamrick.

Chapter 355. *Sixth Generation*

Children of Joseph Green and wife, Sarah Hamrick· Solon married Catherine Hamrick. Andrew Jackson married Permelian Green. Patience Jane married George Green McSwain. Charles Jefferson never married.

Chapter 356. *Sixth Generation*

Children of Asa Lovelace and wife Mary Green. James Louis married Permelia Pruett. Benjamin Franklin married Nancy Green. Major John married Permelia Lovelace, second wife, Susanna Green. Burton Cregg married Mary Bridges. George Washington married Roxanna Pruett. Willis never married. Sarah never married. Judith never married. Nancy never married.

Chapter 357. *Sixth Generation*

Children of James Green and wife, Priscilla McBrayer. Robert Lee married Etta Lee. Susanna married Joseph Hamilton Jones.

Children of James Green and wife, Sarah Beam: Liddie married William B. Wells. Mittie married Charles Lee. Ida not married. Bettie not married. Two infants.

Chapter 358 *Sixth Generation*

Children of Harvey Randall and wife, Eunice Green. Achella married Martha Dedmon. Pinkney married Rosanna Holland; second wife, Gussie Harrell. Shaw married Panthia Hamrick, second wife Anne Hamrick, third wife Claudie Hamrick. Alice

Green married Mary Hamrick. Jacob married Delila Harrell. Samuel Tilden married Lela Harris. Martha married Robert Biggerstaff. Cora married Daw Wilkie. Margaret married Braxton Harrell.

CHAPTER 359 *Sixth Generation*

Children of William Green and wife, Matilda Bridges: John married Cinthia McSwain; second wife Loucindy McSwain. Elvira married John Beason. Crawford married Clementine Lovelace; second wife, Rebecca McSwain. Susanna never married. Boss married ———— ————.

CHAPTER 360. *Fifth Generation.*

Children of David McSwain and wife, Rebecca Cawart· Thomas married Hannah Green James married Mary Wilson. George married Mary Hamrick Nancy married George Green. Jane married William Hamrick Millie married Elijah Hamrick.

Children of David McSwain and wife, Catherine Robertson. Margaret married Elijah Hamrick Elizabeth married David Robertson, (no children).

CHAPTER 361. *Sixth Generation*

Children of James McSwain and wife, Mary Wilson: Sarah Jane married Benjamin Childers. John married Caroline Black. Nancy never married. Eliza Ann never married. Amanda never married Alexander never married. James Matherson never married. Loucindy never married Elvira never married. Mary never married Two infants.

CHAPTER 362 *Sixth Generation*

Children of Thomas McSwain and wife, Hannah Green· George Davis married Eliza Wammac Amos Wright married Mary Allis Hamrick. James Lee married Dora Pruett. Eunice Jane married Hill Hamrick. John never married.

CHAPTER 363. *Sixth Generation*

Children of George McSwain and wife, Mary Hamrick. Catherine married Moses Latham Elizabeth never married.

Children of John McSwain and wife, Mary Hamrick: Elijah married Harriott Jackson Nancy married Elijah McSwain

CHAPTER 364 *Seventh Generation*

Children of Elijah McSwain and wife, Harriott Jackson· John married Mary White. William Ensley married Margaret Isler Joseph Lonlo never married. Samuel Avon married Ruth Hogue. Loucindy married Columbus Mathis Elijah married Ella Carroll. Catherine Jane never married Cynthia Ellen never married Edmond Gaston never married Mary married Kelley Allen. Nancy married Thomas Allen. Rebecca never married. James married ———— Henderson

CHAPTER 365. *Seventh Generation*

Children of Moses Latham and wife, Catherine McSwain: Moses married Mary Biggers; second wife, Jane Mitchell. Mary married Francis Marion Pruett. Nancy Jane married Moses White. Sarah Ann never married.

CHAPTER 366 *Fifth Generation.*

Children of Benjamin McSwain and wife, Rebecca Smith. Benjamin Franklin married Nancy Green, second wife, Judith Green David married Mary Ann Hawkins, second wife, Elizabeth Melina Jones James William married Martha McGinnis. Hassell married Mary Chambers Priscilla married David Freeman. Sarah married James Braddley. Margaret married David Hogue Smith. Dinersey never married. Candace never married. Easter never married. Elizabeth never married.

CHAPTER 367. *Sixth Generation.*

Children of Benjamin Franklin McSwain and wife, Nancy

Green: George Green married Patience Jane Green. Berry Ezell married Nancy Jane Etters; second wife, Narcissus Hessentine Green. Nancy never married.

Children of Benjamin Franklin McSwain and wife, Judith Green: Lenard married Laura Crawley, second wife Susanna Williams. Ellen married Benjamin Kizer, second husband, Monroe Newton. Joseph Enboden married Fannie McSwain, second wife, Sarah Cantrell. Louisa married Nathaniel Lovelace. Candas never married. Margaret never married. Galveston married Alexander Kiser. Benjamin Bussie married Mamie Moore.

CHAPTER 368. *Sixth Generation.*

Children of William McSwain and wife, Margaret McGinnis: Dinersey married John Berry. Loucindy married Moses Cash. Didcamey married Thomas Blackwood. Evy Silvanie never married. Mary never married. Emma never married. Doctor never married.

CHAPTER 369. *Sixth Generation.*

Children of Hasell McSwain and wife, Mary Chambers: Fannie married Joseph Enboden, McSwain. One infant.

CHAPTER 370 *Sixth Generation.*

Children of Jackson McSwain and wife, Ellen Hawkins: Benjamin Franklin mrried Martha Wall; second wife, Lenna Hardin; third wife Roxanna Hamrick. Charles married Laura Lovelace. Adline married Dillard Dobbins. Catherine married James Scruggs. Hannah married Smith Canady. Rebecca married Coley Scruggs. Mary married General Tate. Elizabeth married James Gettis.

Children of Jackson McSwain and wife, Elizabeth Maleney Jones: Penina Ritta married Benjamin F. Cooper. George Griflon married Tillie Webb.

CHAPTER 371. *Sixth Generation.*

Children of David Hogue Smith and wife, Margaret McSwain
Albert married Louisa Guffey   Effie married James Campbell

CHAPTER 372. *Sixth Generation*

Children of David McSwain and wife, Mary Ann Hawkins· Lan-
drumn married Millie Scruggs.   Sina married James Dobbins
Richard married Louvenia Dobbins   James married Fannie Hopper   William married Laura Weathers

CHAPTER 373. *Fifth Generation.*

Children of Gabriel Washburn and wife, Priscilla McSwain
Abriam married Rebecca Durham.   Martha married Gilbert Har-
rell.   Susanna married John Harrell.   Benjamin married Delphia
Philbeck, second wife, Mary Dobson   Gabriel married Emeline
Thompson.   Joseph married Mary McEntire   John married Mary
Ann Magness.

CHAPTER 374   *Sixth Generation*

Children of John Washburn and wife, Mary Ann Magness. Perry
married Elizabeth Henson   Abner married Zinnie Proctor. Ruben
married Sarah Crowder.   Margaret married Robert Crowder   Mary
married William Suttles.   Catherine married William Gold.   Priscilla married Anderson Williamson   Benjamin married ————.

CHAPTER 375   *Seventh Generation*

Children of Perry Washburn and wife, Elizabeth Hinson· Joseph
married Easter Fortenberry, second wife, Narrie Williamson
Thomas B married Carrie Elliott, second wife, Grace Woodruff
Robert Lee married Mildred Carpenter   Narcissus married Peter
McKee.   Rhoda married James Crowder

CHAPTER 376   *Seventh Generation*

Children of Ruben Washburn and wife, Sarah Crowder.   William
married L   M   N   lla married Hester Horton   Allis married

Ruben Bridges (no children). Mary married Tatum Hollifield. Bertha married Oakley Biggerstaff. Daisy married Charles Davis. John never married.

CHAPTER 377. *Seventh Generation*

Children of Anderson Williamson and wife, Priscilla Washburn: Decatur married Martha Elliott. Eliza married Joseph Walker Lafayette married Susanna Gross. Clifton married Elizabeth Mauney. Joseph married Eliza Hord. Pearson married Beamie Blair. Philetus married Minnie Lee Charles. James married Mattie Wells. Johnnie married Julian L. Carson.

CHAPTER 378. *Seventh Generation*

Children of William Gold and wife, Catherine Washburn · Perry married Susanna Covington. Monroe married Adline Wofe. John Oliver married Mary Carroll. Benjamin Franklin married Narcissus Pannell. Robert Crowder married Gatheria Chitwood. Margaret Mauney married Ruben Bridges. Elizabeth Mitchell married Edmon J. Bridges. Mary Ann never married. Missouri Catherine never married. Leander never married. Cicero never married.

CHAPTER 379 *Sixth Generation.*

Children of Abriam Washburn and wife, Rebecca Durham: Charles Gabriel married Earsley Walker; second wife, Sarah Crowder. Margaret married Elijah Eskridge. Priscilla married Edmond J. Lovelace. Mary Jane married Albert Green. Patience married George Green. Thomas never married. Eunice never married.

CHAPTER 380 *Seventh Generation.*

Children of Charles Gabriel Washburn and wife, Sarah Crowder: Willard Winslow married Eliza Harrell. Phoebie Adline married George Washington Hamrick. Rebecca Hessentine married Cleophus Averose Hamrick. Chauncey Abriam married Roseline Harrell; second wife Arrie Estella Hamrick. Patience Priscilla married

Joseph Cabness; second husband. Sidney Hill Hamrick Seaton Allen married Mintie Missouri Hamrick Chivans Averose married Hessentine Irvin Honey Illif married Hannah McMurry. Cora married Coleman Doggett Dennis Gordan married Ella Hamrick Margaret Jane married George Washington Stockton. James Crowder never married Doctor William married Catherine Briscoe. Thomas never married

CHAPTER 381. *Seventh Generation.*

Children of Elijah Eskridge and wife, Margaret Washburn: Thomas Chugman married Permelia Blanton Richard married Mary Judith Blanton Carrie married Robert B McBrayer (no children) Martha married Pinkney Cabness Eunice married Thomas Jefferson Holland John never married Charles never married.

CHAPTER 382 *Sixth Generation*

Children of John Harrell and wife, Susanna Washburn · Housand married Cinthis McSwain Robert married Margaret Wesson. Abriam married Adline Coble Hosie married Caroline Webb. Delphie Street married David McSwain. Priscilla married Henry Champion. Sarah married Isaac Price Thomas married Loucindy Hamrick Nathaniel married Susanna Lovelace. Dicey never married Daniel never married

CHAPTER 383. *Seventh Generation.*

Children of Hosie Harrell and wife, Caroline Webb: William married Fannie Jenkins. Robert Lee married Judith McSwain Charlotte married John Calhoune Hamrick

CHAPTER 384 *Seventh Generation.*

Children of Nathaniel Harrell and wife, Susanna Lovelace · Jane married Crusoe Moss Landis Hosentine married Charles Cabness. Sarah married Newton Landers.

CHAPTER 385 *Seventh Generation*

Children of Thomas Harrell and wife, Loucindy Hamrick. Phoebia married Judson Pettie. Fannie married Franklin Royster Lillie never married

CHAPTER 386. *Seventh Generation*

Children of Robert Harrell and wife, Margaret Wesson George married Ellen McEntire, second wife Carrie Horne James W. married Liddie Moore. John married Carrie Allen. Charles B. married Lillie Dobbins. Allis Victoria married Marshall Beard. Raford Fitzhugh married Clarrie Louis David Abriam never married.

CHAPTER 387. *Seventh Generation.*

Children of Henry Champion and wife, Priscilla Harrell: Amanda married Leander Randall Charlotte married George McDaniel Permelia married ———— ————.

CHAPTER 388. *Seventh Generation*

Children of Isaac Price and wife, Sarah Harrell Louisa married Arthur Wall. Francus married Benjamin Cleary Adline never married. Susanna never married. Permelia married John Lanchaster. John Louis married ———— Butler. Robert married ———— ————. Charlotte married ———— ————

CHAPTER 389. *Sixth Generation.*

Children of Gilbert Harrell and wife. Martha Washburn. Housand married Abie Beam. Street married Sarah McCombs Gilbert married Sarah Jones. Jonathan married Elizabeth Blanton Martin married —— Blanton, second wife, Darcus Dillingham. Nancy married Elijah Blanton. Martha married Neeley Green Lamer married William Kitchins. Frankie married Robert Lankford Priscilla married Gilbert Digh Gabriel married - - Joseph never married William never married.

Chapter 390   *Seventh Generation.*

Children of Housen Harrell and wife, Abie Beam. David married Permelia Harrell   William married Jane Durham; second wife, Louisa Hamrick   Catherine married Samuel Bridges.   Barberry never married.   Elizabeth married Thadus Walker.

Chapter 391   *Seventh Generation*

Children of Gilbert Harrell and wife, Sarah Jones: Elijah Newton married Vianna Blanton   Drury Dobbins married Jane Hamrick.   Martha married Newton Eskridge.   Cinthia never married.

Chapter 392   *Seventh Generation*

Children of Street Harrell and wife, Sarah McCombs·   Mary Ann never married   Loucindy never married.   Ellen never married.

Chapter 393   *Seventh Generation.*

Children of Jonothan Harrell and wife, Elizabeth Blanton   Wesley married Catherine Harriss   Eliza Helen married Drury Lee

Chapter 394.   *Seventh Generation.*

Children of Elijah Blanton and wife, Nancy Harrell: Monroe married Repsey Webb   Materson married Catherine Carpenter. John married Nancy Byers   Sarah Martha married Taylor Webb.

Chapter 395   *Seventh Generation.*

Children of Neeley Green and wife, Martha Harrell·   Martin married Louisa Bridges   Joseph H married Callie Magness.   David married Ollie Dailey

Chapter 396.   *Seventh Generation.*

Children of William Kitchen and wife, Laurdner Harrell.   Gabriel married Sarah Green.   Mary married Alanson Green.   Silverancy married John McFarland   Adline never married   Isabell never married

CHAPTER 397 *Seventh Generation*

Children of Robert Lankford and wife, Frankie Harrell· Aquilla married Mary Walker Love married Loucindy Glascoc. Elzeberry married Sarah Workmen. Walter married Amanda Moore. Genelia married Monroe Morgan. Robert married Hester Lemons. Mary never married

CHAPTER 398. *Fifth Generation.*

Children of Jonathan McSwain and wife, Sarah Norwood. George married Margaret Latham John married Mary Hamrick. David married Elizabeth Hamrick Penina married Samuel Hamrick. Mary never married. Rebecca never married.

CHAPTER 399. *Sixth Generation*

Children of George McSwain and wife. Margaret Latham Margaret married David McSwain. Penina married Jonothan McSwain.

CHAPTER 400 *Sixth Generation.*

Children of David McSwain and wife, Elizabeth Hamrick. Elijah married Nancy McSwain. David married Margaret McSwain. Jonothan married Penina McSwain John never married Sarah never married Mary never married Judith never married. Samuel never married. Catherine never married. Jane never married

CHAPTER 401 *Seventh Generation.*

Children of Elijah McSwain and wife, Nancy McSwain: Mary Elizabeth married Thomas Walker McSwain. James Thomas married Mintie Duncan. Nancy Catherine married Achella McSwain Elijah Hamrick married Mary Price John David never married. Hannah Jane never married. Judith never married. Elizabeth never married.

CHAPTER 402 *Seventh Generation.*

Children of David McSwain and wife. Margaret McSwain: Thomas Walker married Mary Elizabeth McSwain David Andrews

11

OLD TYPE OF SPINNING WHEEL. (SEE PAGE 27)

married Sarah Edwards, second wife, Emeline Champion. Elijah Matterson married Eliza Davis; second wife, Carrie Campbell. Mary married Samuel Edgar Champion.

CHAPTER 403 *Fifth Generation*

Children of John Matheney and wife, Elizabeth McSwain. John married Elizabeth Hamrick. Elizabeth married Nelson Turner. Mary married George Bridges. Jonothan never married

CHAPTER 404 *Sixth Generation*

Children of Nelson Turner and wife, Elizabeth Matheney: John married Sarah Ellis. Emeline married Craton Ledford Jane married Wiley Blanton; second husband, James Champion Arthur married Arkansas Turner. William married Jane Lee, second wife, Prarie Turner Elizabeth married Nathaniel Scoggins. Eliza married Berry Putnam, second husband, Richard Hughes. Richard married Salene Blanton. Eli married Jane Blanton. Sarah married Samuel Young Hamrick Margaret never married. Hovle never married.

CHAPTER 405 *Seventh Generation.*

Children of Craton Ledford and wife, Emeline Turner· John married Elizabeth Glover, second wife, Elmira Jolley. Berry married Adelia Turner. William married Saline Houser. Ambrose married Mary Westbrooks. George married Kisiah Hullender; second wife, Sarah Louis Susanna married John Beam. Jane married Robert Wright Frances married Todge Anthony Two infants.

CHAPTER 406. *Seventh Generation.*

Children of Berry Putnam and wife, Eliza Turner. William married Zilphia Spurlin.

Children of Richard Hughes and wife, Eliza Turner: John Berry married Ada Goode. James married Hannah Matheney; second wife Hassie Hawkins. Clifford married ———.

Chapter 407   *Seventh Generation.*

Children of William Turner and wife, Jane Lee. Ralph married Sarah Bright   Ada married Hackett Wall, second husband, William Putnam.

Children of William Turner and wife, Prarie Turner: Edgar married Emma Randall. Festus married Eva Millwood; second wife, Millie ——— ———. Aaron married Willie Wilkins Tula married John Weaver. Hattie married William Henry Eva married John Pettie

Chapter 408.   *Seventh Generation*

Children of Eli Turner and wife, Jane Blanton· John C. married Margaret Crisp William Perry married Cora Underwood Cleophus married Mandie McCreary. Elizabeth married Alexander B. Lee. Maudie married James Aaron Lee. Hoyle Burton not married Gazzie not married Susanna Lottie not married Dennis Clifton not married. Charles D not married

Chapter 409.   *Seventh Generation.*

Children of Richard Turner and wife, Salena Blanton. Hoyle married Laura Hawkins. Malena married Ransom Hicks. Ida married Robert Lee Jones. Alpha married George Webb Elizabeth married John O Wright Aria married Augustus Bridges. Margaret married Joseph Beam Martha married Emma Rollins Clarence never married.

Chapter 410   *Seventh Generation.*

Children of Arthur Turner and wife, Arkansas Turner William Arthur married Ollie Surratt Alice married Green Surratt Ella married ——— Hope. John married Elizabeth ———.

Chapter 411.   *Sixth Generation*

Children of George Bridges and wife, Mary Matheney: William married M... M... ...   Hassell married Addisey Hicks. Abram married Mary Allen. Lawson married Emeline McSwain. Vianna married Crawford White. Frankie married Carrie Huffstettler. David married Elizabeth McSwain. Mary married James McSwain. Elizabeth married Leander Kindrick. Sarah never married.

CHAPTER 412. *Seventh Generation.*

Children of Lawson Bridges and wife, Emeline McSwain: Harriott married Thomas Camp. Ellen married James Saunders. Martha never married

CHAPTER 413. *Fifth Generation.*

Children of John Matheney and wife, Elizabeth Hamrick: David married Hannah Sarah Hamrick. George married Mary Hamrick. Louis married Tempie Simmons. Sarah married Wiley Hamrick; second husband, George Robertson Hamrick. Rebecca married Alvin Padgett. Mary Elizabeth married William D Gillispie. Hannah married Louis Hawkins; second husband, James Green. Elmira married Thomas Hamrick. Joseph never married. John never married. James Landrum never married

CHAPTER 414. *Sixth Generation.*

Children of David Matheney and wife, Hannah Sarah Hamrick. Cleophas married Hester Scruggs. Eveline married Monroe Hawkins. John married Cinthia Jones. Loucindy married Seaton Green. Bessie married Pinkney Green. Carmelia married George Simmons. Elijah married Penina Green

CHAPTER 415. *Sixth Generation.*

Children of George Matheney and wife, Mary Hamrick: John Landrum married Panthia Tate. Wiley married Ella Tate. George married Louisa Holland.

CHAPTER 416. *Sixth Generation.*

Children of Louis Matheney and wife, Tempie Simmons: Joseph married Clarenda Wall; second wife, Laura Scoggins

Chapter 417. *Sixth Generation.*

Children of William D. Gillispie and wife, Mary Elizabeth Matheney: William married Laucretia Goode. Joseph married Manervia Goode Nancey married Richard Padgett. Catherine married Elijah Lovelace.

Chapter 418. *Sixth Generation.*

Children of Louis Hawkins and wife, Hannah Matheney Toliver married Thaney Goode.

Children of James Green and wife, Hannah Matheney: Clairie Jane married Berry McSwain Padgett. Susanna married Columbus Hoyle.

Chapter 419 *Seventh Generation*

Children of George McSwain and wife, Margaret Latham· Margaret married David McSwain. Penina married Jonothan McSwain

Chapter 420 *Fifth Generation*

Children of Charles McSwain and wife, Margaret Norwood Margaret married Thomas Moore "Red Headed" George never married Black Headed George never married.

Chapter 421. *Sixth Generation.*

Children of Thomas Moore and wife, Margaret McSwain· General married Vesty Victoria Hamrick Elizabeth married Thomas Jolley Martha married Calvin Holland Leah married Leander Jolley Mary married Erasmus Holland Cinthia married Gold Griffon Holland Sarah married David Hamrick Francis married Loucindy O'Neal

Chapter 422. *Seventh Generation.*

Children of Thomas Jolley and wife, Elizabeth Moore· Brivet married Penina Elmore, second wife, Sarah Holland, third wife, Ella Robertson. Stanford married Mollie Durham. Prairie married Julia D...... ... ... Mar. Humphrie Loucretia married

Joseph Hamrick, second husband, Crawford Jolley. Silveraney married Isaac Hamrick. Elizabeth married James Morehead.

Chapter 423 *Seventh Generation.*

Children of Calvin Holland and wife, Martha Moore. Francis never married. George married Julia Haynes. Pinkney married Octavia Fowler. Loucindy married George Bridges; second husband, Thomas Hayne. Julia married Wallace Hopper. General never married.

Chapter 424. *Seventh Generation.*

Children of Leander Jolley and wife. Leah Moore· Hilary married Sarah Hamrick. Caroline married William White Cordelia married Berry Hopper. Sarah married Louis Scruggs. Susanna married Jackson Scruggs Jane never married Zoulia never married Two infants.

Chapter 425 *Seventh Generation.*

Children of Erasmus Holland and wife, Mary Moore: Thomas married Cleary Haynes Elizabeth married Richard Hughes Telitha married Gilford Hamrick. Jane never married.

Chapter 426 *Seventh Generation.*

Children of Gold Griffon Holland and wife, Cinthia Moore: Thomas married Eunice Eskridge, second wife, Jane White Adline married Marshall Newton Hamrick. Permelia married Timmons Gamewell Lee. Sarah married Samuel Robert Haynes. Franklin married Mollie Wall Jane married Roy Morehead Gold Griffon married Allis Champion Mary never married.

Chapter 427 *Seventh Generation.*

Children of General Moore and wife. Vesty Victoria Hamrick· Davie married Elizabeth Lattimore. Marshall married Dovie Blanton Mollie married Charles Putnam Carrie married Lanton Blanto O........i B.... H...l M.g.. rried John

Emch Morehead Aquilla married Coran Blanton. John Matterson married Effie Freeman

Chapter 428. *Seventh Generation*

Children of Francis Moore and wife, Louemdy O'Neal: John married Kisiah Bridges. Thomas married Louisa Pritchard. James married Elvenia Dickey. second wife, Mary Blanton, third wife, Judith Green. Stanley Moore married Jane Hamrick, second wife, Mary Dickey. George married Roseline Blanton. Margaret married George Green. Rebecca never married.

Chapter 429. *Fourth Generation.*

Children of William Champion and wife, Mollie Hamrick. George married Rebecca McSwain, second wife Elizabeth Bostic

Chapter 430. *Fifth Generation.*

Children of George Champion and wife, Rebecca McSwain· Richard married Mariah Burchett.

Children of George Champion and wife, Elizabeth Bostic· Martha married Phillp Davis David married Amelia Jane McBrayer Sarah married Christopher Love India married William Carr McSwain Margaret married William McSwain. George never married Elizabeth never married.

Chapter 431. *Sixth Generation*

Children of David Champion and wife, Amelia Jane McBrayer: Dr. Clifton Otus married Allis Crowder Martha Elizabeth married Thomas C. Pettie

Chapter 432 *Sixth Generation*

Children of Christopher Love and wife, Sarah Champion. James never married George never married.

Chapter 433 *Sixth Generation*

Children of Phillp Davis and wife, Martha Champion. Cham-

pion married Margaret Scruggs. Lola Effie married Samuel Turner.
Sarah Elizabeth married Richard Byers Ida May married George
Simmons. Phillip never married One infant. '

Chapter 434. *Sixth Generation.*

Children of William Carr McSwain and wife, Judith Champion:
George never married James never married.

Children of William Carr McSwain and wife, Margaret Champion.
Rachael never married Rebecca Elizabeth married Crawford Green

Chapter 435 *Fourth Generation*

Children of James Hamrick and wife, Susanna Hamrick George
married Phoebia Wright, second wife, Anna Martin. Susanna married Samuel Harrell Mary married Thomas Hardin. Elizabeth married Samuel Bridges Rebecca married Samuel Bridges

Chapter 436 *Fifth Generation.*

Children of Samuel Harrell and wife, Susanna Hamrick Housand
married Levisey McBrayer Frankie married Robert McBrayer
Rebecca married Martin Beam. Samuel married Leah McBrayer
Priscilla married George Blanton Susanna married James Mc-
Brayer. John married Jane Wray. Cinthia married John Bostic
Amos married Elizabeth Baxter James married Susanna Blanton.
William married Elizabeth Bennix

Chapter 437 *Sixth Generation.*

Children of Robert McBrayer and wife, Frankie Harrell. Amos
married Amanda Strawd (no children) David married Martha
Blanton John married Margaret Lovelace Priscilla married James
Green. Cinthia married Samuel Eskridge, second husbnd, Jesse
Jolley Robert B married Carrie Eskridge, second wife, Amanda
Logan. James never married Susanna never married.

Chapter 438. *Seventh Generation*

Children of David McBrayer and wife Martha Blanton Charles married Pearl Wray. John married Susanna Blanton. Olive married Samuel S Royster.

Chapter 439. *Seventh Generation.*

Children of John H McBrayer and wife, Margaret Lovelace. Robert William married Buena Packard Carrie married George P. Webb. Addie May married William Broadway David Roy not married Edwin Yates not married

Chapter 440 *Seventh Generation.*

Children of Robert B McBrayer and wife, Amanda Logan: Robert married Louise Mallah Corrie married Cletus Hord Ida married William Lawery Loula married Daniel Davis. Logan E. married Fay Young. Stella married Henry Dosier. Mamie married Grover King Mabel married Myrtle Hunneycutt.

Chapter 441 *Sixth Generation*

Children of Martin Beam and wife, Rebecca Harrell. Martin married Dora Harrell John married Doma Strowd Posey married Narcissus Gordan. Amelia married Achillis Durham Priscilla married Joseph Edwards. Mary married Willis McDaniel, second husband, George Doggett, third husband, James Canady. Martha married Crawford Lovelace Sarah married James Green James never married. David never married.

Chapter 442 *Seventh Generation*

Children of Joseph Edwards and wife, Priscilla Beam: Martin Luther married Louisa Bridges Ellen Rebecca married Wilber Day. Doctor Gardner married Jane Davidson, second wife, Barberry Wood Sarah married John Bridges David married Jimmie Bridges James never married Joseph never married

Chapter 443 *Seventh Generation*

Children of Martin Doctor and wife, Amelia Beam. William

Jasper married Margaret Manning. Robert Achillis married Ida Cheek. Mattie never married. One infant.

CHAPTER 444 *Seventh Generation*

Children of Willis McDaniel and wife, Mary Beam: Emma married John Hamrick. Rachelan married ———— Claton.

Children of George Doggett and wife, Mary Beam: Sarah married Jasper Green

CHAPTER 445. *Seventh Generation.*

Children of Posey Beam and wife, Narcissus Gordon· Martin married Lettie Cavney. Charles married Catherine Carlton. William married Minnie Ewart Minnie never married.

CHAPTER 446. *Sixth Generation*

Children of Housand Harrell and wife, Levicey McBrayer: Alfred married Earsley Suttles Susanna married Hoyle Gross William married Esther Suttles. Alburtic married Elizabeth McArthur. James married Sarah White Samuel married Rachael Beam Delila married Thomas Withrow. Edith never married. Elisha never married.

CHAPTER 447. *Seventh Generation*

Children of Alfred Harrell and wife. Earsley Suttles. John married Jane Webb Catherine married Mills Flack Housen married Judith King. Franklin married Nancy Bland; second wife, Julia Edwards Earsley Priscilla married Albert Bridges. Martha married Asa Bowman Judith married Burwell Thorne Josie married John D Long Delila married Barney King. Three infants

CHAPTER 448 *Sixth Generation.*

Children of Samuel Harrell and wife, Leah McBrayer· Permelia married David Harrell. Drucilla married William Harrell. Frankie married John Duncan Lula married John Martin. Cordelia married L... ... ... married Susanna Simmons. John married Fannie Bridges. Amos married Hattie McDaniel; second wife, Daisy McDaniel. Elizabeth married Simeon Duncan. Jesse never married Housen never married.

CHAPTER 449   *Seventh Generation*

Children of John Harrell and wife, Jane Webb Beulah married Logan Moore. Fay married Della Moore; second wife, Sarah Gambell. Maudie married William Moore Flay married Allie Huntley. Emma married Ralph Flack. Bessie married Gordon Young. Fredrick married Burnice Tate. Hoke not married.

CHAPTER 450.   *Seventh Generation*

Children of Thomas King and wife, Sarah Harrell· Robert married Vonnie Fortune Docia married George McDaniel Robus married Lenna Williams. Stanyarn married Nettie Hensley. Cuttie married William Taylor. Della not married Susanna not married Alice not married Fannie not married.

CHAPTER 451.   *Seventh Generation.*

Children of Franklin Harrell and wife, Nancy Bland: Nancy married William Smart.

Children of Franklin Harrell and wife, Judith Webb: Judith married Henry Toney. Patrick married Jesse Hoyle Cleveland married Lucey Hardin Thomas married Ada Brackett. Claud married ———— Freeman. Palmer not married Clovis not married

CHAPTER 452.   *Sixth Generation*

Children of James McBrayer and wife, Susanna Harrell: Lorenzo married Catherine King. Delila married Washington Wilkie Susanna married Franklin Daniels Amelia married Winfield Roach. Jane married John Robbins Dr. John H. married Ida Palmer. Napoleon Bonaparte married Mary Spark-

CHAPTER 453. *Sixth Generation.*

Children of John Harrell and wife, Jane Wray: Lawson married Caroline Price. Dr. John married Hattie Black.

CHAPTER 454. *Sixth Generation.*

Children of John Bostic and wife, Cinthia Harrell George married Margaret Goode. John married Susanna McArthur. Susanna married Henderson Carroll. Nancy Ann married Franklin Moore. Tempie married Andrew McDaniel. Samuel married Jane Suttles.

CHAPTER 455. *Seventh Generation.*

Children of Samuel Bostic and wife, Jane Suttle: Joseph married Attie Hallman. John married Elizabeth Durham Carroll married Mary Beam George Pleasant married Bertha Bryan, second wife, Mary Thornton, third wife, Molena Stover. Louisa married Monroe Putnam. Mary Jane married Samuel Austell. Plato Lee married Annettie Moore. Wade Dobbins married Flora Holloway Attie Texas never married Samuel never married Thomas never married Cinthia Judith not married Orlando married Benna Hamrick

CHAPTER 456 *Seventh Generation*

Children of Henderson Carroll and wife, Susanna Bostic: John married Susanna White. Mary married John Oliver Gold. Johnston married Avelonia McSwain Cinthia married John Byrd. Sarah married Christopher Phillips. Martha married George Henderson. David never married.

CHAPTER 457. *Seventh Generation*

Children of Franklin Moore and wife, Cinthia Bostic. Achella married Margaret Dean John married Nancy Doggett. Susanna married Marshall Carroll

CHAPTER 458 *Seventh Generation*

Children of George Bostic and wife, Margaret Goode: John

married Olavine Smart   Marthia married Samuel Harrell.   Leonard married Cordelia Harrell   Dr. Chivans married Massie Aldridge. Hester married John Carson.   Eugenia married Bailey G. Weathers. Charles married Minnie Wilhart   Georgie married Dr. Robert Garrin   Mary Clarenda never married.   Rodney James never married

CHAPTER 459.   *Seventh Generation.*

Children of John Bostic and wife, Susanna McArthur: Alonzo married Sarah McDonnell.   Arrenia married William Murphy   Milson married Nettie Huntley, second wife. Minnie Hall   Eula May married Ivey Johnston.   Garmilha never married.   Baxter never married.   Docia not married.

CHAPTER 460.   *Seventh Generation.*

Children of Thomas Carroll and wife, Priscilla Bostic.   John married Zoulia McDonnell, second wife, Allie Sorrells. Sarah married John Henry Ford.   Addie married Arthur Harriss   Samuel married Lenard Watkins   James Robert married Lela Martin. Thomas never married   George married.   Charles married.

CHAPTER 461.   *Seventh Generation*

Children of Andrew McDaniel and wife, Tempie Bostic·   Richard married Quintina Hicks.   Cornelia married Jefferson Smith.   Ola married John C. Cowen   Hattie married Amos Harrell.   Charles never married   Grover never married   Doctor never married   Daisy married Amos Harrell.

CHAPTER 462.   *Seventh Generation.*

Children of Washington Wilkie and wife, Delia McBrayer: George married ———— ————   Catherine married Martin Putnam   Jane married Samuel Putnam   Judith married William Taylor.

CHAPTER 463.   *Seventh Generation.*

Children of Leonidas Daniels and wife, Susanna McBrayer: John

UNCLE BERRY HAMRICK
WHO DIED DURING 1918 AT THE ADVANCED AGE OF 98 YEARS. LAST MEMBER OF THE
THIRD HAMRICK GENERATION IN CLEVELAND AND RUTHER-
FORD COUNTIES. (SEE PAGE 11)

married Catherine Webb.   Joseph F. married Ella Beard.   Leonard married Hattie Meseek   Otus never married   Margaret not married.

Chapter 464. *Seventh Generation.*

Children of Lorenzo McBrayer and wife, Catherine King.   Dr. Thomas not married.

Chapter 465. *Seventh Generation*

Children of Winfield Roach and wife, Amelia McBrayer·   James married Mary Green.   Harriss married Jason Hoover   Flossie married Perry Street   Ola married James Hollifield.   Susanna married Lawrence Killian.   Estella married William Putnam   John not married

Chapter 466. *Seventh Generation*

Children of John Robbins and wife, Jane McBrayer·   James married Nancy Cole   John married Sarah Snider   William married Vera Wilson Broadus married Sarah Quinn.   Colon married Etta Green.   George married Cora Holland.   Docia married William Morrow.   Carrie married Phelix Quinn   Lester married Pearl Hopper.   Arnie never married.

Chapter 467. *Sixth Generation*

Children of James Harrell and wife, Susanna Blanton.   Martha married Capt. James Whitten Beam.   Mary married James Lee.   Sarah married Jacob Lorance   James never married.

Chapter 468. *Seventh Generation*

Children of Capt James Whitten Beam and wife, Martha Harrell: James A. married Eliza Chitwood.   Samuel Monroe married Sarah Bridges   Cicero married Susanna McFarland. Solon M. married Elizabeth Harrell   Julius married Emma Harrell   Foster married Fannie Hass; second wife, Hester Thombs   John married Mary Carpenter   Mary Ann married Zecheriah Edwards.   Margaret married George Hamrick.

Chapter 469. *Sixth Generation.*

Children of Amos Harrell and wife, Elizabeth Baxter · Dr Lawson married Margaret Stockton; second wife, Carrie Carmackle. Catherine married Joseph Green   Arrie married Thomas Thombs. Elizabeth married Solon M. Beam. Calvin married Sarah Gettis. Dr John A married Louisa McFarland.   Samuel married Mattie Bostic   George never married.   Bate never married   Susanna never married.

Chapter 470. *Sixth Generation*

Children of William Harrell and wife, Elizabeth Bennix   Martin married Vianna Webb. Robert married Catherine Suttles   Housen married Martha King   Mary Ann married Anonymus Weir. Eveline married Posey Lynch   Rebecca married James Weir.   George married Bell Sigenalder; second wife. Emma Oliphant.

Chapter 471. *Seventh Generation.*

Children of Housand Harrell and wife, Martha King: Joseph married Mary Dellinger.   Zoiah married Mary Burgess.   Mittie married Winfield Grider   Effie married Burwell Moore.   Judson never married.   Jordon never married.   Pearl never married

Chapter 472. *Seventh Generation.*

Children of Robert Harrell and wife, Catherine Suttles: George married Lucy Homes.   Julia married William Collins. Sarah Jane married William James Hilton.   Carrie married Jacob Metcalf. Charles married Nancy Bailey   Martha married Leander Smith. Carrie married William F Wilson.   Barney married Edna Jankiss; second wife, Margaret Grigery.   Julius married Ella Ruppe; second wife, Candas Harbruner. Lillian married Gladstone Gatling. Eugene never married   Daisy never married.   Alice never married.

Chapter 473. *Seventh Generation.*

Children of Martin Harrell and wife Vianna Webb·   George married Coro   · ~ · h Priscilla married Columbus Campe Hughie

12

married Susanna Norrells   Catherine married Colon Lorence. John
Bell married Gussie Rollins   Margaret married Albert Mauney.
William never married.

CHAPTER 474. *Seventh Generation*

Children of Posey Lynch and wife, Eveline Harrell: Leander
married Loula Elliott   Jane married Albert Holland.   Graham
married Arrie Smith.   Minnie married John Sorrells   Marcus
married Edna Jackson.   Erastus not married.   Martha not married

CHAPTER 475   *Seventh Generation*

Children of Samuel Harrell and wife, Rachael Beam   Charles
married Lillie Grigg   Angus married Eva Hufstettler   Alexander married Allie Sigmon. Cleveland married Gussie Sigmon   Gussie
married Pinkney Randall   Thomas married Pearl Hope   Henry
married Vancy Bridges.   Mary married Palmer Kindrick   Catherine not married.

CHAPTER 476   *Seventh Generation*

Children of Dr John H McBrayer and wife, Ida Palmer, Troilius
De Costa never married   William Garlan married Mamie Goodson   Phernia married Ernest White.   James Harrell never married   Mary Susanna not married   John not married

CHAPTER 477   *Seventh Generation*

Children of Dr. John Harrell and wife, Louisa McFarland   Gaston married Ellen Gettis.   Cansas married Batie Harrell

CHAPTER 478   *Seventh Generation.*

Children of Calvin Harrell and wife, Sarah Gettis·   Lawson
married Amanda Thacker.   Panthia married Demcrov Edwards
Lillian married Jesse Sparks.   Elizabeth married Landrum Lee.
Susanna not married.   Plato never married   Sarah not married.

CHAPTER 479. *Seventh Generation*

Children of Albertie Harrell and wife, Elizabeth McArthur: Alfred married Margaret Wease. Judith married Curtis Watson Levicey married Arthur Bridges Sarah married Franklin Wease. Delila married Joseph Allen. Bell married Oscar Padgett Shippard married Mary Wells Carson never married

CHAPTER 480. *Seventh Generation*

Children of Hoyle Gross and wife, Susanna Harrell. Luther married Dona Moore. Julia married Pinkney Martin Alpha married John Wommac; second husband, Thomas Cole Hester married John Jones Sammie married Pinkney Jones. Phillip married Mary Ledbetter. Vernitia married George Young Housen never married Loucasy never married. Calvin never married

CHAPTER 481. *Seventh Generation*

Children of William Harrell and wife, Ester Suttles· David married Biddie Price Jane married Warlie Walker Housen married Seneth Goforth Samuel married Jane Walker. Pleasant married Minnie Wagler. Etta married William Bailey Bascum Carson married Margaret Randall. Batie married Carrie Blanton James married Carrie Cooper Dobbins never married Homesley never married

CHAPTER 482. *Seventh Generation.*

Children of Thomas Carson and wife, Delia Harrell: Henry Clay married Hattie Wells. Marcus married Blanch Harrell. John married Hester Bostic Mary never married Allis not married Florence not married.

CHAPTER 483. *Seventh Generation.*

Children of Tahomas Withrow and wife, Priscilla Harrell: Weldon married Goldie Dagger Alice married John Kisbr. Bell married Jabez Hopper. Debbie married Joseph Green. Thomas married Dollie McMahan. Georgie married Clarence Hodge. James married —————— ——————.

CHAPTER 484 *Seventh Generation.*

Children of James Lee and wife, Mary Harrell: Laura married William Jones; second husband, Ruben Wilson Jones Quinn never married.

CHAPTER 485. *Seventh Generation.*

Children of Jacob Lorance and wife, Sarahann Harrell: Lanton married Mary Jane Palmer. Esley married Julia Peeler. Colon married Catherine Harrell.

CHAPTER 486 *Seventh Generation.*

Children of John Beam and wife, Donie Stroud Charles married Ola Blackworth William not married Carrie not married Maggie not married Forest not married.

CHAPTER 487 *Seventh Generation.*

Children of Mills Flack and wife, Catherine Harrell· Carney married Walter Wilson. Otto married Cleo Mauney Effie married Arthur Young. Susanna married Joseph Elliott. Two infants.

CHAPTER 488. *Fifth Generation.*

Children of George Hamrick and wife, Phoebia Wright: Wright married Ellen Peeler James Young married Catherine Hardin. Loucindy married Winston W. Wright Judith married Charles Blanton. Malindy married Hood Jolley Elizabeth married Richard Hughes Candas married Young Hughes

CHAPTER 489. *Sixth Generation.*

Children of Wright Hamrick and wife, Ellen Peeler: George Washington married Phoebia Adline Washburn Mary married Andley M. Lattimore Sarah married Webb Eskridge. Mintie Missouri married Seaton Allen Washburn Amanda never married. Phoebe married Kinch Hamrick

CHAPTER 490. *Sixth Generation.*

Children of James Young Hamrick and wife, Catherine Hardin:
Charles Jefferson married Sarah Hamrick. Susanna married Elijah
McSwain. Loucindy married Thomas Harrell. Andy married Sarah
McSwain. Oliver never married. Henderson Newton never married.
Sarahann never married.

CHAPTER 491. *Seventh Generation.*

Children of Charles Jefferson Hamrick and wife, Sarah Hamrick:
James Young married Cansas Ellen Byers. Elijah Bly married
Gallena Green. Catherine married Solon Green. Oliver Newton
married Almedia Pruett.

CHAPTER 492. *Eighth Generation.*

Children of James Young Hamrick and wife, Cansas Ellen Byers:
Fredrick Delmire married Natley Harris. Fitzhugh B married
Ollie Green. Charles Doggett never married. Vasser Huffman
married Beuna Green. Myrtle Esmer married Clarence Hamrick.
Euzelia married J. Andrie Barry.

CHAPTER 493 *Eighth Generation.*

Children of Elijah Hamrick and wife, Gallena Green: Octa
Foy married Edwin Hamrick. Carroll married Mary Etta Moore.
Charles Rush married Georgie Grice. Dr James Yates married
Elizabeth Champion. Oliver Paul married Jessie Pangle. Clifford
Laddie Watts not married. Elijah not married.

CHAPTER 494. *Eighth Generation.*

Children of Solon Green and wife, Catherine Hamrick. Garland
Manning married Maudie Osborne. Gertrude not married.

CHAPTER 495. *Seventh Generation.*

Children of Andy Hamrick and wife, Sarah McSwain: Elizabeth
never married

Chapter 496. *Sixth Generation*

Children of Winston W. Wright and wife, Loucindy Hamrick. George Washington married Biddie Robertson. Abner Benson married Eunice Durham. Susanna married James Hamrick. John married Sarah Bridges. James married Laura Batie. Thomas married Martha Jenkins. Joseph Pinkney married Margaret Jolley. Phoebia married Franklin McEntire; second husband, Stephen Humphries. Judith married Granderson S. Ramsey. Mary married Drury McDaniel Harrell. Parthia Nittia married Marion Eskridge.

Chapter 497. *Seventh Generation.*

Children of George Wright and wife, Biddie Robertson. Georgeanna married Willie E. Fite.

Chapter 498. *Seventh Generation*

Children of John Wright and wife, Sarah Bridges: Martin married Margaret Harrell. Blanche married Lawson Bridges. Beuna married Crowder Philbeck. John O. married Elizabeth Turner. Clyde married Ellen McDaniel.

Chapter 499. *Sixth Generation*

Children of Young Hughes and wife, Cadance Hamrick. Cinthia married Drury McDaniel. Sarah Manervia married William F. Jones. Loucindy married Pinkney Martin. Toliver never married. Elmira married Elias Putnam.

Chapter 500. *Seventh Generation.*

Children of William F. Jones and wife, Sarah Manervia Hughes: George married Sarah Mitchell. Andy married Elizabeth Ruppe; second wife, Emeline Harrell. Pinkney married Sammie Gross. Albert married Laura Ruppe. Nancy married James Owens. John married Hester Gross. Robert never married.

Chapter 501. *Fifth Generation*

Children of Thomas Hughes and wife Mary Hamrick: George

married Mary Harrell; second wife, Martha McSwain. Jesse married Hannah Irvin. Edmon married Cinthia Gage. William married Artie Webb. Hosie married Sarah Hamrick. Susanna married Asa Lovelace. Annie married John Neal. James never married. Elizabeth never married.

CHAPTER 502. *Sixth Generation*

Children of George Hardin and wife, Mary Harrell: Delphia married Samuel Bridges; second husband, Berry Hamrick. Sarah married Dobbins Hamrick; second husband, John Horne. Caroline married David Hamrick; second husband, Isam Owens. Artie married Samuel Putnam.

Children of George Hardin and wife, Martha McSwain: Nancy married Willis Webb. Amanda married David Oliver Green. Saleny married Anderson Owens.

CHAPTER 503. *Seventh Generation.*

Children of Samuel Putnam and wife, Artie Hardin: Monroe married Louisa Bostic. John D. married Mary Jones. William married Zoulia Bridges; second wife, Ida Turner; third wife, Eva Hughes. Benjamin Franklin married Eliza Spangler. Clifton married Panthia Jones. Gordon married Esther Poston. Pinkney married Sarah Wallace; second wife, Edith Parker. Tilden married Novella Eskridge. Mary married John Gold. Rachael married Perry Wellmon. Esther married Wade Elliott. Charles married Mollie Moore.

CHAPTER 504. *Seventh Generation.*

Children of Willis Webb and wife, Nancy Hardin: Drury Dobbins married Rosanna Dycus. Victoria married John Jesse Jones. Martha married Albertie Melton.

CHAPTER 505. *Seventh Generation.*

Children of Anderson Owens and wife, Malena Hardin: George married Barberry Bridges. Arrie married Lensey Bridges. Alonzo married Dovie Burns   Julious married Hettie McDaniel   Clinton not married.

Chapter 506. *Seventh Generation.*

Children of John Horne and wife, Sarah Hardin: John married Docia Harrell   James married Hattie Jenkins   Susanna married Victoria Lovelace, second husband, Cicero Bridges.

Chapter 507   *Sixth Generation*

Children of Jesse Hardin and wife, Hannah Irvin· John married Martha White. Zillie married James Philbeck (no children). Lenna married Benjamin Franklin McSwain (no children). Jane married W Perry Lovelace   Eunice married Elijah Edmon Jones. Rachael never married   Abriam never married   Irvin never married

Chapter 508. *Seventh Generation.*

Children of W. Perry Lovelace and wife, Jane Hardin: Allis married Daniel Brooks.

Chapter 509. *Sixth Generation.*

Children of Edmon Hardin and wife, Cinthia Gage· Anonymus married Susanna Butler. Berry married Jane McDonnell. Drilla married Joseph Harmon   Susanna married McCager Doggett. Noble never married

Chapter 510. *Sixth Generation*

Children of William Hardin and wife Artie Webb· Asa married Mary Wilson   William Jackson married Hettie Clark   Deaney married William Green   Susanna married Drury Phillips. Jesse married Caroline McClure. James married Elizabeth Downey; second wife, Fannie Goode; third wife, Octavia Haynes. Jane married Samuel Melton   Sarah married John Cooper   Mary married George Smith   Priscilla married David Forbus   Artie married William L   married Alfred Harmon   Catherine married William Keeter   Zecheriah married Mollie Efler.   John married Nancy Upchurch.   George never married.

CHAPTER 511.   *Sixth Generation.*

Children of Hosie Hardin and wife, Sarah Hamrick: Jesse married Narcissus Holland; second wife, Artie Bridges.   Catherine married James Young Hamrick.

CHAPTER 512.   *Sixth Generation.*

Children of Asa Lovelace and wife, Susanna Hardin.   James married Judith Hamrick   Edmon J married Priscilla Washburn. William Brison married Sarahann Harris; second wife, Liddie Sapoch.   Thomas married Judith McSwain   Berry married Mary Bridges.   Susanna married William McDaniel.   Mary married Samuel McSwain; second husband, Robert Mintz.

CHAPTER 513   *Seventh Generation.*

Children of James Lovelace and wife, Judith Hamrick: Drury S. married Priscilla Lee.   Permelia married Major John Lovelace Hannah married Perry Pruett.   Jane never married.   Adline never married.

CHAPTER 514.   *Seventh Generation.*

Children of William Brison Lovelace and wife, Sarahann Harriss· Asa Monroe married Cordelia Hamrick, second wife, Susanna Wilkins   Junius married Ellen Lee.   Margaret married John H McBrayer.   Louisa married Larkin Arkansas McSwain   Victoria married Zacheriah R Walker.   Cora married Dr. Timmons Greenberry Hamrick   Clementina married Crawford Green   Docia married Haden Wall   Pinkney never married   Elvira never married.   One infant   Dr. Thomas married Carrie Wilkins

CHAPTER 515.   *Seventh Generation*

Children of Berry Lovelace and wife, Mary Bridges·   Cicero married Dora Hawkins   Victor married Susanna Horne

CHAPTER 516. *Seventh Generation.*

Children of Thomas Lovelace and wife, Judith McSwain: Crawford married Sarah Boggs first, he next married Martha Beam Eunice married Smith Wilkins

CHAPTER 517. *Seventh Generation.*

Children of William McDaniel and wife. Susanna Lovelace: George married Dovie McDaniel Susanna married Zebulon Whitaker. Kisiah married Jabez Hamrick. James never married

CHAPTER 518 *Seventh Generation.*

Children of Edmon G. Lovelace and wife, Priscilla Washburn· Allis married Thomas Kennedy Barnett.

CHAPTER 519 *Seventh Generation*

Children of Anonymus Hardin and wife, Susanna Butler: Perry married Susanna McDonnell William married Harriott Reaves. Jane married Lawson Wright Doctor married ———— Gossett. Julia married ———— ————.

CHAPTER 520. *Seventh Generation.*

Children of Asa Hardin and wife, Mary Wilson. Brison married Mary Scoggins. James married Priscilla Phillips. Spencer married Julia Scoggins Monroe married Susanna Padgett. George married Cintha Price Nancy never married Sarah never married. Susanna never married. Jane married ———— ————.

CHAPTER 521 *Seventh Generation*

Children of Drury Phillips and wife, Susanna Hardin: Martha married Franklin Goode Mary Ann married Decatur Hardin Priscilla married James Hardin. Sarah married Tanner Street. Martin married Susanna Pintuff Monroe married ———— Pintuff.

CHAPTER 522. *Seventh Generation.*

Children of Jesse Hardin and wife, Caroline McClure James married Martha Hill. Alonzo married Narcissus Thombs. Harris married Malissa Burgin. Samuel married Loucindy Kiser Jane married Charles McCraw Lillie married Cardis Morrow' Bell married Garfield Burgan Ada married Ezell Hamrick William married ———— Smith. Buster married ———— Smith. Alberta married Susan Hardin.

CHAPTER 523. *Seventh Generation.*

Children of James Hardin and wife, Elizabeth Dawning: Lafayette married Margaret Moore; second wife, Rebeckey Gordon. Doctor married Francis Good; second wife, Margaret Street Susanna married Richmond Hardin

Children of James Hardin and wife, Octavie Holmes· Posey married David Davis, second wife, Mary Millwood George married Allis Lynch; second wife Minnie Pool, third wife, Elisabeth Mintz Joseph married Jane Irvin John married Mary Holhfield. Priscilla married James Horne. Sarah married Jefferson Dawney. Delila married James Hollifield. Martha married Philip Funderburk

CHAPTER 524 *Fifth Generation.*

Children of Samuel Bridges and wife, Elizabeth Hamrick: David married Rebecca Gutrie. Aaron married Liddie Scruggs. Alexander married Hettie Daves; second wife, Elizabeth Walker Jane married Claybourne Blanton Frankie married Isam Owens. Mary never married Moses never married William never married

CHAPTER 525 *Sixth Generation.*

Children of Isam Owens and wife, Frankie Bridges: Andy married Judith Green. Priscilla married Carver Hamrick. Willis married Louisa Blanton; second wife, Dicey Dycus Jane married Berry Green Wiley never married.

CHAPTER 526 *Sixth Generation.*

Children of Alexander Bridges and wife, Hettie Daves Samuel

married Mary Logan. Jane married George Davis. Elizabeth married Drury Robinson. Priscilla married Willis Green. Biddie married Harvey Hohfield Sarah married William Lovelace. Margaret married Jesse Wells George married Loucindy Holland. Loucindy never married.

CHAPTER 527. *Seventh Generation*

Children of Willis Owens and wife, Louisa Blanton: Wiley married Fannie Hollfield Willie married Jane Hollifield Charles married Malissa Ramsey Asa married Jose Guffee. Priscilla married Thomas Robbins Marendy married Elijah Bridges Hessie married Charles Nodine.

CHAPTER 528. *Seventh Generation*

Children of Samuel Bridges and wife, Mary Logan: Amose married Laura Bridges Smith married Carrie Green Elijah married Marindy Ownes Mills married Fannie Hamrick. Lensey married Arrie Ownes Caleb married Fannie Bridges. Marcus married Zoudie Ledford. Barberry married George Ownes Mindie married Columbus Alexander Jones Effie married Thomas Melton Two infants

CHAPTER 529. *Seventh Generation.*

Children of George Davis and wife, Jane Bridges: Carney married Laura Culbreth Mamie Seaton married Blanch Walker Martha married Landrum Hamrick Arrie married Taylor Dobbins. Ida married Eli Davis Loucindy married Charles Padgett Hessie married Robert Wells. Mina married Edgar Bridges Georgie not married. Narcissus not married

CHAPTER 530 *Third Generation*

Children of Moses Richard Hamrick and wife, Mary Bridges. Henry married Elizabeth Bowens Sarah married Perry Green Magness. J   married S   Hamrick Price married Nancy

Bridges. Enoch ——————. Jeremiah —————— Nathaniel ——————. Thomas ——————. Susanna married
James Hamrick

CHAPTER 531. *Fourth Generation*

Children of Price Hamrick and wife, Nancy Bridges· Moses
married Sarah Robertson. John married Elisabeth Robertson.
Richard married Mary Wall. Sarah married Hosie Hardin. Mary
never married.

CHAPTER 532. *Fifth Generation.*

Children of Moses Hamrick and wife, Sarah Robertson Street
married Elmira Bridges. Amose married Diser Edwards Robert·
married Nancy Hamrick. Andy married Susanna Hamrick.
Marion married Frankie Bridges Artie married Washington Bridges.
Jane married Burwell McSwain (no children). Narcissus married
Paxton Davis Lucretia married John Tate Lucinda married
Joseph Padgett. Eli never married. Moses never married Rich-
ard never married.

CHAPTER 533. *Sixth Generation*

Children of Street Hamrick and wife, Elmira Bridges: Marshall
Newton married Adline Holland Sidney Hill married Elizabeth
Harrell, second wife, Patience Priscilla Washburn John Calhoune
married Charlotte Harrell Leander Sheppard married Sarah Ham-
rick Wiley Cicero married Paold Turner Alonzo Marion married
Eleanor McMurry

CHAPTER 534 *Fifth Generation*

Children of Paxton Davis and wife, Narcissus Hamrick: George
married Jane McSwain Elizabeth married Price Hamrick. Mc-
Duffie married Sarah Webber John married Zoulie Bridges. William married Hester Lee Mary Ann married John Arnell Martha
married James Gipson. Emeline never married Thomas never
married.

REV. G. P. HAMRICK,
WIFE AND SON

CHAPTER 535. *Fifth Generation.*

Children of Price Hamrick and wife, Elizabeth Davis: Chancey Gidney married Loucindy Bailey. Martha married Oliver Butler; second husband, Charles Bailey. Mary married Leander Butler. Darcus married Samuel Wilson. Carrie married Edgar McCurry. Margaret married Edgar Moore.

CHAPTER 536. *Sixth Generation.*

Children of McDuff Davis and wife, Sarah Webber: Charles never married. Russell never married. Franklin never married. Cecile not married. Mandy not married.

CHAPTER 537 *Sixth Generation.*

Children of John Tate and wife, Laucretia Hamrick· Andrew married Cinthia McSwain (no children) Etta married Jefferson Pruett.

CHAPTER 538 *Sixth Generation.*

Children of Marion Hamrick and wife, Frankie Bridges. Sarah never married.

CHAPTER 539. *Sixth Generation*

Children of Amose Hamrick and wife, Dizer Edwards: Monroe married Elizabeth Bright. Margaret married Thomas Bridges.

CHAPTER 540 *Sixth Generation*

Children of Alonzo Iredell Hamrick and wife, Nancy Hamrick· Jane married Avery Smith. Hester married Joseph Wesson Emma married John Cleary. Martha never married.

CHAPTER 541 *Sixth Generation*

Children of Andy Hamrick and wife, Susanna Hamrick William Moses married Susanna Blanton Two infants.

Children of George Bowen and wife, Susanna Hamrick. Augustus married Elizabeth Brackett Ella married Haxton Suttle.

Chapter 542. *Fifth Generation*

Children of John Hamrick and wife, Elizabeth Robertson: Elijah never married. Steeley never married. Eunice never married. Elizabeth married Benjamin Bowens. Mary married Green Bowens.

Chapter 543 *Sixth Generation.*

Children of Benjamin Bowens and wife, Elizabeth Hamrick. Susanna married Isaac Randall Elizabeth married George Pinsan. Jane married Calvin Bowens. Mary married Gabriel Hamrick.

Chapter 544. *Fifth Generation*

Children of Richard Hamrick and wife, Mary Wall: Price married Elizabeth Davis Gabriel married Mary Bowens, second wife, Lela Bishop; third wife, Margaret Arrowood Thomas married Christine Ledford Nancy married Alonzo Iredell Hamrick. Amanda married Van Wallace. Elmira married David Grant.

Chapter 545 *Seventh Generation.*

Children of Marshall Newton Hamrick and wife, Adline Holland: Barnett Edgar married Bessie Fortune Burrus Olan married Ola Whisnant Dora married William Jennings. Della married Hackett Blanton Emma married S O Andrews. Beuna married Arlando Bostic. Grover Cleveland not married. Ollie not married.

Chapter 546 *Seventh Generation*

Children of Sidney Hill Hamrick and wife, Elizabeth Harrell: Belvey married Charles Jefferson Hamrick. Darfer married Hershall Blanton Ida not married.

Children of Sidney Hill Hamrick and wife, Patience Priscilla Washburn: Phocian Hines not married Bernice not married.

Chapter 547. *Seventh Generation*

Children of John Calhoun Hamrick and wife, Charlotte Harrell:

Gillet Vanhes married Emma Ledbetter. Grover Thurman married Bertha Harrell. Garvin Street not married. Wake not married.

Chapter 548   *Seventh Generation*

Children of Leander Sheppard Hamrick and wife, Sarah Hamrick: Spurgeon not married. Otto Vetus married Carrie Maze. Alger Vason married Etta Abernathy. Ruben Hubbard not married. Vilus Fitzhugh not married. Broughton never married.

Chapter 549   *Seventh Generation*

Children of Wiley Cicero Hamrick and wife, Paola Turner: Wait Caralile married Florence Martin. Volena married Ralph Cline. Ethel married George Threadbill. Lyman not married. Alma not married. Helen never married.

Chapter 550   *Seventh Generation*

Children of Alonzo Marion Hamrick and wife, Ellenora McMurry: Evans married Laura Jones. Dewitt married Buna Hawkins. Twitty married Minnie Brooks. Neeter married Winslow Jones. Darcus married Cleton Humphries. Bula married Besalan Hamrick. Elmira not married.

Chapter 551   *Seventh Generation.*

Children of George Davis and wife, Jane McSwain. Ida married Kish Hambright. Thomas married Docia Peeler. Margaret married Edgar Batie. Lola married John Williams Oates. Clifton married ———— ————

Chapter 552.   *Seventh Generation.*

Children of John Arnell and wife, Maryann Davis: Lottie married Bunyan Jones. Duffie not married.

Chapter 553   *Fourth Generation.*

Children of Hour Hamrick and wife Elizabeth James. James
13

married Nancy Hopper   Elizabeth married James Ellison   Jane never married. Nathaniel never married.

CHAPTER 554   Fifth Generation.

Children of James Hamrick and wife, Nancy Hopper· Benjamin married Fannie Roberts; second wife, Martha Morris   Monroe married ——— ——— Mary married William Cox   William Adolphus married Mary Lowery, second wife, Martha Byers, third wife, Panthia Green. Amanda married Alonzo Turner. Lorenzo Daw never married. Levincey never married. Cordelia never married   Julian never married. Walter never married   Eveline married ——— ———.

CHAPTER 555.   Fourth Generation.

Children of Nathaniel Hamrick and wife, Mary Bowens. William David married Martha Padgett   Sarah married Jackson Gipson (no children).

CHAPTER 556.   Fourth Generation

Children of Enoch Hamrick: Mary married Clator Smith.

CHAPTER 557.   Sixth Generation.

Children of Clator Smith and wife, Mary Harrill· Landrum L. married Nancy Diana Hamrick. Charles C. married Sarah Francis. Susanna Jane married James Doggett; second husband, Samuel Poston. Kisiah married John Yarborough   Sarah Martha married Watson Lee, second husband, Albert Moorehead. Samuel Amose married Sarah B. Cooper. Nancy never married.

CHAPTER 558.   Seventh Generation.

Children of Charles C. Smith and wife, Sarah Francis: Avery married Jane Hamrick; second wife, Margaret Glasgoe   Mary married Noble Hamrick   Josephine never married

CHAPTER 559. *Seventh Generation.*

Children of Samuel Amos Smith and wife, Sarah Cooper Blakeman married Elizabeth Giles Franklin married Fannie Marshall Hill married Jane Bowens. William never married.

CHAPTER 560. *Seventh Generation*

Children of Samuel Boston and wife, Susanna Jane Smith: Miller never married.

CHAPTER 561. *Seventh Generation.*

Children of John Yarborough and wife, Kisiah Smith: Louis married Jackery Grigg. Emma Allison never married Allis never married. Fannie married Joseph Quinn. George never married. Wade never married.

CHAPTER 562. *Seventh Generation*

Children of Watson Lee and wife, Martha Smith: Melvenia married James Henry Blanton.

Children of Albert Morehead and wife, Martha Smith: George married Callie Hawkins.

CHAPTER 563. *Fourth Generation.*

Children of Perry Green Magness and wife, Sarah Hamrick: Benjamin married Elizabeth Mauney; second wife, Nancy Walker. Jacob married Edith Webb Susanna married Thomas Hawkins Samuel married ——— Ragan William never married. Robert married Mary Wilson.

CHAPTER 564. *Fifth Generation.*

Children of Benjamin Magness and wife, Elizabeth Mauney: William married Susanna Eskridge. Maryann married John Washburn.

Children of Benjamin Magness and wife, Nancy Walker: Samuel married Nancy Grigg Robert married Susanna Grigg second wife,

Mary Whisnant. Joseph married Hettie Beam. Sarah married Franklin Goode

Chapter 565. *Sixth Generation*

Children of Robert Magness and wife, Mary Whisnant. Samuel Coon married Anabell Henry George married Lillie Poston. John married Bonnie Morrow. Cora married James Austell. Benjamin never married. Robert never married

Chapter 566 *Sixth Generation.*

Children of Samuel Magness and wife, Nancy Grigg: Ruphus L. married Hester Crowder. Mary never married Crowell never married

Chapter 567 *Sixth Generation*

Children of Franklin Goode and wife Sarah Magness· John married Susanna Allison Martha married Harvey Richards. Sarah Susanna married John McCurry. Nancy married Harry Jones Elizabeth married Levi Watterson. Mary married Jason Bridges Joseph never married. Martin never married Emma never married Thomas married ———— ————.

Chapter 568 *Sixth Generation*

Children of Joseph Magness and wife, Hettie Beam: Judson married Elmira Surratt Mary married William Jones Sarah married William Horne David married Elizabeth Whisnant. Catherine married John Tisdell Benjamin never married Perry never married. Jane married James Elliott.

Chapter 569. *Fifth Generation.*

Children of Jacob Magness and wife, Edith Webb: Benjamin married Susanna McBrayer, second wife, Adline Sweezy; third wife, Martha Clark. Sarah married William Chitwood Eliza married W···· ··· McN·····

CHAPTER 570. *Sixth Generation.*

Children of Benjamin Magness and wife, Adline Sweezy: Alonzo married Elizabeth Mayhan   Robert married Jane Byrd.   George married Mary Jackson, second wife, Allis Levington.   Elijah married Mollie McDonnell.   Elmira married John McFarland.   Susanna married William B. Palmer.   Jacob Perry married Bell Adams.

Children of Benjamin Magness and wife, Martha Clark   John married Mary Barber.   William married Annettie Edwards.   Martha married Franklin M. Martin.   Julia married J. W Adams   Benjamin married Rillie Kennan.   Hue married Lucy McDonnell.   Leand married Walter Murphy.   Gertrude married H. D Ellen.   Bonnar married Willie McDonnell.   Amanda married J. W. Fetzer.

CHAPTER 571. *Sixth Generation.*

Children of William Magness and wife, Susanna Eskridge·   John married Allis Neal   Jacob married Ella Chitwood.   William married ————— Parker.   Callie married Joseph H. Green.   Jane married Gaither Philbeck.

CHAPTER 572. *Sixth Generation*

Children of William Chitwood and wife, Sarah Magness·   Eliza married James A Beam   Julia married David D. Whisnant.   Alpha K. married Julians Lattimore.   Elizabeth married Columbus C. DePriest.   Susanna Edith married Franklin Lattimore

CHAPTER 573. *Eighth Generation.*

Children of Decatur Williamson and wife, Martha Elliott. Charles married Hester McMurry.   Narrie married Joseph Washburn.   Erastus never married   Hattie Josephine married Harris Mauney.

CHAPTER 574. *Eighth Generation.*

Children of Joseph Walker and wife, Eliza Williamson: Eugene Edward   ···i · T····a T·····u·.   M· ·t· ····j·l Franklin L

Hoyle Weldon married Selma Beam. Claxter married Johnnie Sites. Vashti married Robert Wilson. Delphan married Loula Edwards Tonce married Charles Wells. Morgan Decatur married Cassandra Piver. Priscilla not married Hugh Anderson not married.

Chapter 575   Eighth Generation

Children of Perry Gold and wife, Susanna Covington: Robert married Georgie Bridges. Agness married James Mack Henson Ola married Lester McCormack Mandie married William Noblet. Florence married Charles Hopper. George married Minnie Padgett. William never married Abbie never married.

Chapter 576.   Eighth Generation.

Children of Benjamin Franklin Gold and wife, Narcissus Parnell: Coleman married Eva Beam. Martin married Fannie Blanton Eva married Joseph Thomas Bridges Allis married James Crawley. Elisabeth married Wayne Covington Pender married Essie Mode. Victor married Vader Humphries Catherine married Clifton Cooper. Ida not married Claudie not married.

Chapter 577   Eighth Generation.

Children of Monroe Gold and wife Adline Wolf· Daniel married Pearl Hamrick. Mattie married G. W. Sheppard Margaret married C. O Barnett. Edmannev married R C. Boyd. Naucey married L. V. Henson Elisabeth married A. E Cross. Agathia married J. J. Stone Samuel married Nola Griffith Thomas married Mattie B Cartwright. Dossey never married Johnnie never married. Emmalee not married

Chapter 578   Eighth Generation

Children of Thomas Green and wife, Susanna McSwain: James David married Jane Ledbetter. William Thomas married Barbara Finettie ⁊ ⸱ ⸱

CHAPTER 579. *Sixth Generation.*

Children of Berry Hamrick and wife, Catherine Hamrick. Crawford married Susanna Bridges. Louisa married Wilson W. Bridges. Nancey married Zecheriah Bridges. Elijah Reuben married Loueasey Bridges. Asa Cicero married Sarah Elizabeth Bridges. Margaret married Noah Green. Cleophas Avarose married Hessentine Washburn; second wife, Fannie Doggett, third wife, Lula Lattimore. George never married. Monroe never married. Sarah Jane never married. Patience never married. One infant.

Children of Berry Hamrick and wife, Cealey Pannell: Thero Plato married Fannie Green. Sipero Adron married Sarah McCluney. Ricey Gatheria married Joseph Green. Ira Estella married Chancey Abrian Washburn. Patria Ida married John Lee.

CHAPTER 580. *Seventh Generation.*

Children of Crawford Hamrick and wife, Susanna Bridges: Enoch Avery married Susanna Owens. Phoebia married Alexander Campbell.

CHAPTER 581. *Seventh Generation*

Children of Zacheriah Bridges and wife, Nancy Hamrick· Cicero Miller married Janes Harrell, second wife, Carrie Hawkins. Eliza married Wm. Benj. Green.

CHAPTER 582. *Seventh Generation.*

Children of Elijah Ruben Hamrick and wife, Louisa Bridges. Toliver Batie married Nola Bridges. Alonzo Martin married Addie Lattimore. Ella married Dennis Gordon Washburn.

CHAPTER 583. *Seventh Generation*

Children of Wilson W. Bridges and wife, Louisa Hamrick· Asberry married Sarah Harrell, second wife, Genelie Cosner. David Posey married Octavia Bridges. Martha married Quinn Brown. George married Augusta Robbins. Hannah married John Stewart. Catherine married William Abernathey. Mary married Henry Bla-

ELIJA B. HAMRICK

lock. Louisey married Newton Brown Elizabeth married John Crawford. Thomas married Fannie Fisher. Gaither married Mary Villinger. John married Bertha Ellis. James never married.

CHAPTER 584. *Seventh Generation*

Children of Asa Cicero Hamrick and wife, Sarah Elizabeth Bridges. James Landrum married Elizabeth Green. Effie married Elisha Edgar Jones. Grover married Suna Hutchins. Lotta never married Clarence never married. Catherine not married.

CHAPTER 585. *Seventh Generation.*

Children of Noah Green and wife, Margaret Hamrick· Docia married John Landrum Hamrick.

CHAPTER 586. *Eighth Generation.*

Children of David Oliver Green and wife, Cassie Hamrick· William Benjamin married Eliza Bridges Martha married Julians Green. Thomas married Lonie Laton. Asa married Lola Hawkins. Nancy married Greenberry Hamrick Judith married Aseph Green. George married Mary Props Charles married Lillie Orr. Cora married Thomas Chambers. Nola married ——— Lowery. John Lane never married. James never married Eight infants.

CHAPTER 587. *Seventh Generation.*

Children of James Hughes and wife, Elmira Ledbetter· Elbert married Eunice Jane McSwain. Andrew married Eliza Hawkins, second wife, Evalee Collins. Berry married Jane Gillispie. Elizabeth married John Gillispie. Catherine married William Chesser

CHAPTER 588. *Seventh Generation.*

Children of William Ledbetter and wife. Eunice Winborne: William married Hester Hawkins. Clearenda married Bankston Bridges. Hessentine married Webb Hawkins

CHAPTER 589. *Eighth Generation.*

Children of Elijah Green and wife, Judith Hamrick. James married Susanna Parris. Aseph married Judith Green. Eliza married Leander Duncan. Salena married Andy Overcash. Beatrice married Edgar Overcash, second wife, Minnie Godfrey. Melchiah married Narcissus Cooper, second wife, Elmer Overcash. Nancy married Andrew Prichard.

CHAPTER 590 *Seventh Generation*

Children of James Bedford and wife, Elizabeth Byers. Seth married Martha Spurlin. Nancy married Anderson Bridges. Elizabeth married Lafayette Wells. Martha married Greenberry Bridges.

CHAPTER 591 *Seventh Generation.*

Children of Greenberry Bridges and wife, Martha Bedford. Sarah married Monroe Beam. Mary Ellen married James E Glover. Seth G. married Octavia Walker.

CHAPTER 592 *Seventh Generation*

Children of Drury Green and wife, Elizabeth Bridges. James married Etta Bridges. Francis married Alice Price

CHAPTER 593 *Seventh Generation*

Children of Seth Bedford and wife Martha Spurlin. Seth married Laura McDaniel.

Benjamin Hamrick, who came from Ireland, had two brothers who came with him. Their names were Robert and Charles. They all served in the Revolutionary War and all lived to be very old men. Benjamin Hamrick had seven children—three sons James, John and Marshall; four girls, Catherine, Polly, Salathy and Selety.

Elder John Hamrick, son of Benjamin Hamrick who came from

Ireland, was twice married. His first wife was a Mozley His second wife was Nancy Todd His first wife had five children, two boys and three girls The names of the boys were Benjamin and Jeremiah, the girls were Catherine, Eliza and Simmedy. The children of the second wife were three boys and two girls The boys were James P., William and Marshall, the girls were Peggy Ann and Emeline. Ten children in all and whom they married.

Benjamin married Peggy Redic. Jeremiah married Lou Childs. Catherine married Jones Crowder Eliza married William Huse. Simmedy married Lebron Pitts Peggy Ann married Thomas Laseter. James P married Malinda Horsley. William married Nancy Cook. Marshall married Edith Hamil. Emeline married Augustus Oliver.

I do not know the names of all their children, but will give all I know. Benjamin Hamrick, son of Elder John Hamrick, grandson of Benjamin Hamrick, who came from Ireland, married Peggy Redic They only had one son, named William I do not know the names of his girls.

Jeremiah Hamrick, son of Elder John Hamrick, married Lou Child Their first child was a boy named John

——— Hamrick, daughter of Elder John Hamrick, married Lebron Pitts. They only had one child, Jane.

William Hamrick, son of Elder John Hamrick, married Nancy Cook. They had four children—one girl named Eliza; the boys were William, John and Joe Benny.

Marshall Hamrick, son of Elder John Hamrick, married Edith Hamil They had five children: three boys, John, Dock and Cicero, two girls, Cordelia and Victoria.

James P Hamrick, son of Elder John Hamrick, married Malinda Horsley They had six children—four boys, James M. Hamrick, C. C. Hamrick, J F Hamrick and W L Hamrick; two girls, Georgia Ann Hamrick and Tarpie T. Hamrick

James P. Hamrick, son of Elder John Hamrick, and grandson of Benjamin Hamrick, who came from Ireland, married Malinda Horsley Had six children. four boys and two girls. Their names and whom they married·

J M. Hamrick married Syntha Fordham. Georgia Ann Hamrick married James Pollard Dr C C. Hamrick married Mattie Creech. J. F. Hamrick married Nancy Creech W L. Hamrick married Lizzie Hoflin. Fannie L. Hamrick not married.

James M. Hamrick, son of James P. Hamrick, grandson of Elder John Hamrick, great-grandson of Benjamin Hamrick, who came over from Ireland, married Syntha Fordham. They had nine children, six boys Benjamin Franklin died in infancy. D M Hamrick, A. W. Hamrick, B Z. Hamrick, O E. Hamrick. S. F. Hamrick, and three girls. Mattie, twins, Minnie and Ninna.

D. M. Hamrick, son of James M. Hamrick, grandson of James P. Hamrick, and great-grandson of Elder John Hamrick, great-great-grandson of Benjamin Hamrick, who came over from Ireland, married twice. First wife, Lula Todd They had three children— two boys, Ernest and Custer. The girl is named Annie. The second wife was Mattie Joiner They had one child, a boy, J D

Annie Hamrick. daughter of D M. Hamrick. granddaughter of James M. Hamrick, great-granddaughter of James P. Hamrick, great-great-granddaughter of Elder John Hamrick and great-great-great-granddaughter of Benjamin Hamrick, who came from Ireland, married Hosey Danley. They had one child. which died in infancy.

Mattie Hamrick, daughter of James M. Hamrick, granddaughter of James P. Hamrick, great-granddaughter of Elder John Hamrick, great-great-granddaughter of Benjamin Hamrick, who came from Ireland, married Americus Jackson They had five children—three boys, R D and Caspus, the other boy died in infancy. The girls are Cara Bell and Claudia.

R. D. Hamrick. son of D M Hamrick grandson of James M.

Hamrick, great-grandson of James P Hamrick, great-great-grandson of Elder John Hamrick, and great-great-great-grandson of Benjamin Hamrick who came from Ireland, married Mrs Stella Roney. They had one child, which died in infancy

A W Hamrick, son of James M Hamrick, grandson of James P. Hamrick, great-grandson of Elder John Hamrick, great-great-grandson of Benjamin Hamrick, who came from Ireland, married Eliza Hare. They had eight children. I do not know their names.

Professor D Z Hamrick, son of James M Hamrick, grandson of James P. Hamrick, great-grandson of Elder John Hamrick, and great-great-grandson of Benjamin Hamrick, who came from Ireland, married Rosa Harper They have no children.

O. E Hamrick, son of James M Hamrick, grandson of James P. Hamrick, great-grandson of Elder John Hamrick, and great-great-grandson of Benjamin Hamrick, who came from Ireland, married Texas Hall They have six children. four boys, Doster, Lindon, Bonney and Chester The girls are Lucy and Vera.

Minnie Hamrick, daughter of James M. Hamrick, granddaughter of James P Hamrick great-granddaughter of Elder John Hamrick, and great-great-granddaughter of Benjamin Hamrick, who came from Ireland, married M. L Patterson. They had five children: two girls, named Violet and Thelma The boys were named Lester, Martell and Willard. Violet married Ike Hyde.

Ninna Hamrick, daughter of James M. Hamrick, granddaughter of James P. Hamrick, great-granddaughter of Elder John Hamrick, and great-great-granddaughter of Benjamin Hamrick, who came from Ireland, married Oscar Lee They have five children—four boys, named Olinthus, Curtis, Robert and S B The girl is named Gladys.

S F Hamrick, son of James M Hamrick, grandson of James P Hamrick, great-grandson of Elder John Hamrick, great-great-grandson of Be____ H_____ ___ ____ from Ireland ___ at the age of nineteen, with pneumonia. This is all of James M. Hamrick's children and grandchildren.

Dr. C. C Hamrick, son of James P. Hamrick, and grandson of Elder John Hamrick, great-grandson of Benjamin Hamrick, who came from Ireland, married Mattie Creech. They only had one child, daughter of Elder John Hamrick, and great-granddaughter of Benja-which died in infancy

Fannie L Hamrick, daughter of James P Hamrick, grand-Hamrick, who came from Ireland

Georgia Ann Hamrick, daughter of James P. Hamrick, and grand-daughter of Elder John Hamrick, and great-granddaughter of Benjamin Hamrick, who came from Ireland, married James Pollard. The names of their children and grandchildren·

Arthur Pollard lives in Texas, married Hattie Blidsole.

Charles Pollard married Joeanna Brown; had five children. Luther, Homer, Jim Tom, Katie and Gidie

John Pollard married Bertha Churchwell, had one child named James.

Mattie Pollard married John Mozley. Had seven children Minnie, Arthur, Ella, Willie, Thomas, Eva and Fannie.

Ella Pollard married William Hendrick. Had four children: Annie, Jewel, Grady, and I do not know the name of the other.

Addie Pollard married Henry Justice. Had four children. Annie, Alvin, Bascom and Sadie

Fannie Pollard married Emmett ———.

Fannie Pollard married Emmett Dixon. Had six children: Thelma, Bertie, Willie, Mattie, Harold and Clyde.

The names of Frank Hamrick's children, grandchildren of James P. Hamrick, great-grandchildren of Elder Hamrick, great-great-grandchildren of Benjamin Hamrick who came from Ireland

James P. Hamrick, son of J. F. Hamrick, married Esther Underwood. They live in Oklahoma and have no children.

Ida Hamrick, daughter of J. F. Hamrick, married Allen Carroll. Had one child named Annie.

Selma Hamrick, daughter of J F Hamrick, married Frank Grice. Do not know their children.

Emma Hamrick, daughter of J. F. Hamrick, married Mark Jackson Had one child, Mattie.

W. L. Hamrick, son of James P Hamrick, grandson of Elder John Hamrick, grandson of Benjamin Hamrick, who came from Ireland, married Lizzie Heflin, had five children: James R., William J., Walter A. The girls are Fatie C. and Mollie.

Walter A Hamrick, son of W. L. Hamrick, and grandson of James P. Hamrick, great-grandson of Elder John Hamrick, and great-great-grandson of Benjamin Hamrick, who came from Ireland, married Cathie Forehand. They have no children.

Mollie Hamrick, daughter of W. L. Hamrick, and granddaughter of James P. Hamrick, great-granddaughter of Elder John Hamrick, great-great-granddaughter of Benjamin Hamrick. who came from Ireland, married Sam Neal. They have two children, named William Byron and a girl, named Martha Washington.

All the parties above named are in Georgia and Alabama This is a copy of a letter written by Fannie Hamrick, Dothan, Ala., Route No 1.

CPSIA information can be obtained at www.ICGtesting.com
Printed in the USA
LVOW03s1336030414

380168LV00006B/477/P